DAWN PATROL

PETER BUNNETT

Michael Terence
Publishing

First published in paperback by
Michael Terence Publishing in 2020
www.mtp.agency

ISBN 9781800940345

Cover image
Peter Bunnett

Cover design
2020 Michael Terence Publishing

Foreword

My story starts in May 1979 when I decided to join the Police.

Many stories have been written about the service, these stories do not always enhance the Police, but the truth is sometimes stranger than fiction. Most stories reach the television screens as serialised stories, they are not usually true, based on some incident in the writer's distant past, and remembered with only a small amount of truth. The story relates to a Police service with non-stop action, which sometimes it is, but mostly it is not, it is a job whose sole purpose is to help the public and prevent crime. I feel sure the reader will appreciate how the Police work, as the book progresses, hopefully appreciating the job the officers carry out, no doubt thankful that they are there. Having completed 30 years' service, I can confirm not every day was lived at a breakneck pace, some days were quite boring, but you had to take the rough with the smooth.

My story takes the reader to Greenham Common, during the time when protests were a regular occurrence, giving the officers long night shifts, and abuse from the ladies present. After this, we were required at Handsworth, in the Birmingham area, ready to quell the disturbances in the town, as we were trained PSU officers. For the uninitiated, this meant we had trained to deal with riots, using the shields if so required, along with long batons, this will be mentioned later in the book. Although Greenham

Common took up a great deal of our time, something else happened in 1984 which took up even more of our time, for those who can go back that far, it was, of course, the miners' dispute. This dispute lasted a full year, the PSU was sent from Thames Valley, but I will discuss this fully in a later, hopefully, you can wait that long. I appreciate the miners had a different point of view, no doubt placed in their minds by their illustrious leader, Arthur Scargill, but I saw incidents at first hand, including the allegation from Arthur Scargill that he was hit with a police shield, which would have been difficult, he was too far back from the shield units, being protected by his minders. The story was intended to work in his favour, I suppose it did when it kept being repeated. There are many stories in this book, unlike Arthur Scargill being hit by a shield, these stories are true.

One

I was living in Plymouth when I decided to join the Police Service, I applied to three separate forces, which you could do in those far off days, they were Thames Valley, the Metropolitan Police, and the City of London Police. I did not apply to Devon and Cornwall, where I was living at the time, there was at that time a good reason for my decision, that reason no longer exists. My first interview was with the Metropolitan Police, this was quickly followed by Thames Valley, both provisionally accepted me, I was pleased with both interviews but I needed to decide. It is now over forty years since those applications were made, I am still awaiting a response from the City of London, I think I am over the age limit now, but it is strange that my application was completely ignored. I would like to thank the City of London for their keen interest in me. I had an important decision to make, it was not easy, but I decided, my choice was Thames Valley. It was an area of the country I knew fairly well, mainly because I spent the last 14 months of my RAF service at RAF Benson.

My Police training was to take place at Eynesham Hall in Oxfordshire, it was a place that had something of a reputation, not a particularly good one, it was also an all-male training school. There were several females employed at the school, they worked in the kitchens, none of them was young, they all had a kitchen smell about them, usually a Brussel sprouts smell. As far as the cooking staff were concerned, I soon found out their skills in the kitchen left much to be desired. There was nowhere else to eat, these meal times had to be endured.

I cannot remember exactly how long the course lasted, I believe it was about four months, these were split into weekly courses, which had an examination at the end of each week. Each of these exams had to be passed before the student could move on, those who failed the exam had a chance to retake it, all of those in the class either passed the first time or passed on the retake, all the class moved forward. The week was spent studying one specific subject, although it was more complicated than that. A prime example was The Theft Act, which covered Burglary, Robbery, and other offences associated with Theft. This particular Act was very important to the constable on the beat, I remember using the Act on many occasions during my career, the majority of these offenders were of course shoplifters, stealing came under that Act. The idea of learning all the Acts was to familiarise himself so we knew when a wrongdoing had occurred, many of the Acts were never used, but they came up in examinations, the Deer Act was one. I learned the Deer Act, but never had a need to use it, there was little in the High Street in the way of deers running wild, but I was ready if it ever happened. Whilst at the training school, there were certain practical tasks to be taken on by all students, they related to subjects we had studied, so it became time to put these subjects into practice. Once the officer took on the practical demonstration, the rest of the class watched his progress, at the end, the class was asked to comment, it was to assist the person carrying out the practical. It worked very well, nobody was trying to embarrass their friends, advice was accepted without question, and taken on board. The important part of particular Acts, was the power in each act given to the officer, something he would find useful in most situations. We began to find out we had a lot of powers, enough to deal with most things that we were likely to come across. I cannot remember what my practical task was, but I passed it, which was something of a blessing, there were not many things on the course that were a blessing. The course itself was interesting, it was difficult at times, as the law is at all times, but it was a great way to learn the law in detail.

The weekly exams took place on the Monday morning, which was a sensible idea, it gave everyone the chance to revise over the weekend, not that everyone needed that time, as I was to find out. A friend of mine had no need to revise, he had what is known as a photographic mind, he never forgot anything he was told, he proved that in his exams, not surprisingly he finished top student.

I kept in touch with my friend and saw him climb through the ranks, he retired as a Superintendent, a well-deserved officer. During our stay at the training centre, my friend and I both stayed at the weekend, all the other recruits went home, they lived a lot closer than I did, my friend was good enough to stay and keep me company. During those weekends we played a lot of tennis, we both improved our game in leaps and bounds, I did some revision as well, which was important for me, although my friend did no revision at all.

The one thing I remember quite vividly was the ritual carried out at mealtimes, we all stood to attention behind our seats, then we were told to sit before getting our food, it was a little like being back at school, with one exception, the food was atrocious. I wish I could pick out a meal which I enjoyed, but that was impossible, all the meals were bad, they were either overcooked or undercooked. If only the cooks had found that in between way of cooking, they may have produced something edible.

During the first couple of weeks we were billeted in the main house, it was like a country mansion. I believe there were four men rooms, it was very comfortable. Following a short stay of only a couple of weeks, we were moved from the house into huts outside the house, they were Nissan type huts, only two students to a room. As far as I can remember these huts were wooden, no doubt very cold in the winter months, but we moved into these erections in late May, it was therefore not that cold. I do recall the ablutions were something of a disaster, I will not comment on that anymore. I was sharing with a student from Essex called Paul, we got on very well. I believe I was the oldest student in our class, this did not worry me too much, I had seen something of life, including service in the RAF. Several of the younger students asked my advice, that was connected to life and not the Police Service, I knew nothing of the Police, but I was quite knowledgeable about life.

There was a long driveway at the house, it led up to the house from the main road. It was not unusual to see students walking up and down the drive during the evening, this was not for exercise, the reason was more important than that, they were simply revising the huge amount of definitions we had to learn. It was not an easy task, the walk seemed to help, some recited the definitions, others kept it to themselves, whatever method was used it did seem to help the process.

There was a fitness side to our stay, although to be fair it was not that rigorous. There was a six-mile run that had to be completed in a specific time, everyone did it in the time, I cannot remember what the time was, but it allowed everyone to finish successfully. I was reasonably fit when I went to the training school, this showed up in the run, I finished second out of sixty students, not back for someone of my age.

There was another strange thing that was taken on board by the students, there was a bar in the house, but it was not for students, this was where the instructors relaxed after a long day in the classroom. Over the weekend there was a duty Sergeant in the house, he was kind enough to open the bar to those students who remained, there were only the two of us, we took advantage of his kind offer. I cannot remember if we went to the local village for a drink, I think that was a possibility, or maybe we just stayed in and revised, I cannot be certain of that fact.

I do remember that when we arrived at the house, entering by the front door, we were informed that was the only time we would use the front door during our stay, there must have been a back way in, but I am having difficulty remembering those days.

There was one practical that all students had to complete, an important one as it happens, this was giving evidence in court, something we were all going to carry out during our career. We had a short piece of evidence that we all had to memorise, then a proper magistrate was brought in from the outside world, she listened intently as we swore the oath and gave our memorised evidence, the evidence was the same for everyone. Once you had finished the

Magistrate commented, it was both enlightening and useful, I do not remember what she said about my effort, I do not think my evidence giving was a problem. Having attended court on many occasions during my career, I believe my evidence improved over the years.

We had to march everywhere, although our marching was not of the same standard I had been part of in the services, but I do not think the instructors expected that, although our class contained eight ex-servicemen, which brought our standard up. There was a Drill Cup at the end of the course, which not surprisingly we won, not that anyone was too bothered, our instructor seemed pleased. The day of the final exam arrived, it was a combination of all we had done on the course, it was a little unnerving, there were rumours about failing, under those circumstances, you were booted out. We did not find out if that was true, everyone in our class passed.

We were able to relax after the final exam, soon we would be saying farewell to all those we had met from different forces, it was sad but life must go on, I was pleased to be leaving training school. The next step was to return to our own Force, where we would attend a one week course, it was called Local Procedure, it was to learn about the way Thames Valley dealt with things. It was an enjoyable week, mainly because there was no exam at the end. I do remember the bar catered very well to our needs, something we had been without at Eynesham Hall. It was while I was at the training school I was informed of my posting, I would be going to Chesham, not a town I was familiar with, but go there I must.

My First Posting

I had known of my posting for some time, although I had no idea where it was until I checked the map. I had been allocated a Police house in the nearby town of Amersham, which I had visited with my brother prior to my posting. Once the training course had finished I took up my posting in Chesham, where I would be tutored by an experienced officer, it was normally for a month, but circumstances sometimes changed that, as it did for me. I was tutored for just two weeks, the officer who was tutoring me took me to as many different situations as possible. It was normal procedure for someone being tutored to attend as many different locations and offences as possible, that gave the officer a wide spectrum of what he was likely to deal with in the future. It was a good system to learn as much as possible, and put what knowledge you had obtained from training school into practice, although doing the job for real was a lot different from what training school had taught, but you learn from all experiences. My tutoring started on my first shift, which was from 2 pm until 10 pm, it is the shift most officers detested, but I did not know that at the time. Every job that came into the control room was offered to my tutor first, he usually accepted it so off we went. I did not get any arrests in those first two weeks, but I dealt with many traffic accidents, and traffic offences, not classed as traffic accidents.

My first arrest was a shoplifter, which I attended with another officer, they were usually easy to deal with, particularly if they stuck to the rules, that meant going to court and pleading guilty. I soon found out that some shoplifters, although seen by the store detective taking an item, then leaving the shop without paying, still wanted their day in court, pleading not guilty to the offence. Some of these people were persistent thieves, the magistrates knew who they were, and punished them accordingly. My shoplifter had stolen a bottle of whiskey from a well-known supermarket, he had been watched by the store detective, she knew who he was, and subsequently arrested by me. We stood outside the shop to wait for transport to the station, the shoplifter asked politely if he could have a drink of whiskey, from the bottle he had just stolen, he seemed surprised when I refused his request. He behaved quite well in the station, he was then placed in a cell to sleep off his drunkenness, he was pleased about that, he slept for several hours before he was charged with the theft and released from custody. He went to court and pleaded Not Guilty, but the magistrates knew him quite well, I know they found him guilty but I cannot remember his sentence, maybe he got a few months in prison because he was a persistent offender.

One of the worst parts of Police work is attending sudden deaths, those are deaths where there is little medical history before the death, these are usually heart attacks, although not in all cases. My first sudden death was an elderly gentleman who had died in his comfy chair in the sitting room, the reason for his death is unknown at that stage. The Police's job is to inform the family of the death, not the most pleasant of tasks, to fill in a form which was passed to the coroner, then get the body removed to the mortuary. The funeral director came to pick up the body, occasionally we helped them in their task, he requested my help on this occasion, it was to remove the gentleman's clothing, which I agreed to do. The gentleman was wearing braces, which we undid, at least we thought we had, but we had not undone them successfully. As we tried to remove his trousers, the braces sprung up and hit the man's testicles, we all cringed at the thought, he on the other hand did not move.

I remember trying to remove a gentleman who had died in the bath, but he had been in the bath all night, thereby making his skin a little loose on his body, we eventually got him out but it was a difficult removal. I had a probationer with me at the time, I thought it might be a good experience for him, he did not think so, he cursed me all the way back to the station.

The one sudden death I remember the most happened on Good Friday, it was in fact a suicide as well. We were called to a house in a relatively expensive part of town, the neighbour had reported it. We went to the house and found this gentleman hanging from the rafters in the loft, it was not a pleasant sight. We had to wait for the doctor to turn up before we could take him down, he confirmed death, which a doctor has to do, although we knew he was dead it is the doctor who signs the form. The neighbour was helpful, stating that the man's wife and daughter had gone to Scotland to see the wife's parents, her husband had to work, that was the reason he did not go. We found paperwork on the downstairs table that appeared to tell the whole story. The husband had been made redundant on Thursday, his wife and daughter were already in Scotland, it was unlikely she knew about his redundancy, but we found something else which related greatly to what had happened. There was a charge sheet from Good Friday, the man had been charged with Drink Driving, no doubt drowning his sorrows from being made redundant, but it all added up to a very sad case. It was a few years later that my daughter told me the daughter was in her class, she was only seven years old.

One of the things that was required of a probationary constable was to attend a Post Mortem, I do not think it is a requirement these days, but I cannot be sure of that fact. When I attended the Post Mortem, there were two other officers present, but they stayed some distance away, very close to the door. The doctor carrying out the event was a well-distinguished man in his field, one of the best in the country I believe. It was not something I would wish to attend regularly, but on this occasion it was interesting, the doctor explained everything he was doing, my colleagues were too far away to be impressed either way. I was fortunate never to attend another Post Mortem, I did not feel it was necessary to attend more than once.

Following my two weeks of tutoring, I was let loose on the public, there were certain things I noticed, I felt I was being watched, I now know that was not true, but it felt like I was the centre of attention in the street. I think all officers feel that way initially, it does take a while to accept and to pass the feeling of being the centrepiece of the street. It took several weeks to appreciate the public were not watching me, they took notice that I was there, but that was all, it is a feeling only policemen get.

He was a local character in the town, there were several, but he was the one who came out at night, he was always aware of which officers were on the street, but he had his uses. He took on his own foot patrol in the town, this was normally in the outskirts, but occasionally he appeared in the town, checking on officers patrolling the street. He would telephone the station if he saw a light on in a factory, or he saw anything he did not think was right. He never stole anything, he never tried to steal anything, but he was always there, not a nuisance, more of an irritation. One evening I walked down the town centre, checking the shop doors as I went, he was on the opposite side of the road, about 20 yards behind. I reached a clothes shop at the end of the High Street, I tried the door and it opened, this triggered the alarm which was very loud, the character watching my actions sped away up the High Street. I think he thought I was going to arrest him, it certainly panicked him. He was someone we thought was not quite the full shilling, he did get involved with other elements in the town, causing him to be sent to prison, I am not sure he would cope with that, I never saw him again as I moved from the town.

There was a nightclub in Chesham called Stages, why it had that name, I never found out, not that I was really that interested. I do not think it is there now, but it might be as I have not been in the town for over 20 years. This club was packed at weekends, kicking the clientele out at 2 am, it was basically an after-hours drinking club, allowing the drunks to carry on drinking. Those officers on duty sat outside in cars to await the 2 am throwing out time, it was an interesting event. There was a small dance floor upstairs in the club, as a result, both men and women attended the club, but that was not the only peculiarity of the place, the women came out in groups, followed by the men. It appears that it was not the place to chat up the women, nobody came out in couples, it did make me wonder about the menfolk. There was never any trouble, we were there as a deterrent, the inhabitants of the club sometimes decided to dance in the street, this took place once they knew the police were there. I also felt we should have recorded these dance sessions, then show it to them when they sobered up, but knowing the calibre of the men that frequented the club, they would probably thought they were suave and sophisticated. My only conclusion was that the men of Chesham had no interest in the women in the club, they were only interested in drinking until they fell over, which many of them did, sometimes during their dance routine in the street. I enjoyed being sat outside Stages, it gave the police a lot of entertainment.

I recall one individual being arrested, he was not keen to go to the police station, but he was eventually bundled into the car and taken the two hundred yards to the nick. In the station car park he refused to get out of the car, he was forcibly removed. The arresting officer then dragged him to the station door, pulling him along the tarmac car park. I noticed he was wearing a leather jacket, it concerned me that it could be damaged dragging him across the car park. Once inside the station, he was asked to remove his jacket before being interviewed, which he did without question. Once he was interviewed he was charged and told he could leave, the arresting officer stood behind him and held onto his jacket, when he released his hand I understood the reason, the jacket was ripped right up the back. He left with a two-piece jacket, no doubt a complaint was going to arrive at the station, once he had sobered up, anyone in his position would complain. I do not know if the complaint was forthcoming, or what the result was.

I was on foot patrol in Chesham one night, it was about 2 am when I received a call from the station, a member of the public had seen a man climbing into a window at the Chesham Tool Hire property, the window was across from a sloping roof, not easy to get into. I went to the premises and met up with a colleague there. I decided to climb up the sloping roof and into the broken window on the first floor, my colleague stood by in case I needed some assistance. I got into the property once I opened the broken window, it was full of large cardboard boxes, they appeared to be empty, I noticed this as I moved them from my path. I saw a man curled up in the corner, he probably thought he was invisible. I shone my torch on him and he recognised the fact I was a police officer, he spoke before I could question him.

"I saw a man climb in so I followed him, I hoped I would catch him," he said.

I decided to respond to the burglar, trying to be as polite as possible.

"I tell you what, I have a look for this man, if I don't find him you're under arrest for burglary, do you understand that?" I said.

He was not happy, he thought I had swallowed his tale about following a man into the room, fortunately, I was not as stupid or as gullible as he was.

We eventually extracted the man from the room and placed him in the police vehicle, he was taken to the station and I awaited the key holder, who was somewhat shocked with the burglary, particularly as the room was empty apart from a load of empty boxes. He also told me there was no way down to the shop from that room, the door was padlocked on the shop side. I went back to the station and interviewed the burglar, but he refused to change his story, he tried to convince me he was doing a good turn, he was charged with burglary and bailed. I cannot remember what his punishment was, but I do know he pleaded guilty at the magistrates' court, someone had obviously advised him, a sensible move. The room in which I found our man was about ten-foot square, what his intention was when he found out there were only empty boxes I do not know, I do not think he had thought that far ahead, in fact, thinking was a problem for him.

The Police Station was in itself a strange place to work, some of the Senior Officers were very finicky, one, in particular, liked checking the registers, he would ask questions about the Property Register, they were questions you could not answer, which was what he wanted. I think it made him think he was superior, I thought he did not have enough to do.

While at Chesham I carried out my CID attachment, every probationer did this, it was a way of finding out if you might eventually want to be in that department, a Traffic attachment came later. My first day I went for a walk up the town with the DS, that was short for Detective Sergeant, we did not travel too far, we stopped at an electrical store. The owner said something to the DS, we then walked into the back office, a bottom drawer was opened and suddenly there was a bottle of whisky on the desk. Two glasses were found and a drink was put in each, it was just after 2 pm, I downed my drink as I thought it was expected, it appeared to be a good move at the time. I was invited to the pub that evening, along with the rest of the CID office, where they chatted to the criminal fraternity, something that did not happen years later. CID officers were later banned from pubs while on duty, I think this followed a spate of drunkenness from certain officers. The majority of good CID officers did not get drunk, it was the bad ones that drank too much. It was also the end of CID officers chatting to criminals in their own environment, it also ended CID officers having loads of informers, the pub allowed this to happen, when going to the pub stopped, so did the informers.

I was invited to the pub again one evening, but I reluctantly turned the offer down, because my shift was about to finish, and I knew it would be a long night in the pub. The DS insisted I go to the pub, he told me to put it down as overtime, he said he would sign the overtime form, which he did. This showed me that CID in those days made up their own rules, but they were effective officers, they got more arrests than uniform, mainly because they knew the criminals intimately. I was glad I did my CID attachment at that time, that CID was about to change forever. The thing I remember about this attachment was the amount of time spent in the pub, but it did bring results, CID officers were respected by the criminals. I dealt with a lot of minor crimes, but I was not allowed to deal with anything too tricky, which was understandable, I lacked the experience of my CID colleagues.

The DS told me a story, he swore it was a true story, I had no reason to think otherwise, he also gave the impression of being an honest man. He was out one night, in his own time, visiting a lady friend, which meant he arrived home in the early hours. He decided not to wake his wife, he entered the bedroom shoeless, started to take off his trousers, for some unknown reason his wife woke up.

"Where have you been to until this hour?" she said in a somewhat angry voice.

He then started to pull up the trousers he was originally taking down.

"I haven't been anywhere, I'm just getting up to go to work, it's an early start, we have an operation on," he said.

He said she took a moment's thought and went back to sleep; the incident was never mentioned again, much to his relief.

My time on CID was interesting, I had a lot of respect for the officers working in that department, apart from their drinking ability, they got results from their endeavours.

A short while later a decision was made to close Chesham Police Station, it was intended we move to the larger station at Amersham. Chesham was going to be used by the beat officers, but all other departments moved to Amersham. Our new station, which was in fact a newer station that Chesham, already had the Traffic department based there, the cell block was a lot bigger, hopefully, it would not take long to fill. The only downside of the move was that most of the trouble happened in Chesham, in saying that Amersham was only a few miles away.

Police Officers who were stationed at Chesham.
The closing party – everyone enjoying the station for the last time.

No sooner had I arrived at Amersham, back on shift having finished my CID attachment, it was time for a Traffic attachment, this was to prove more exciting than I had imagined.

My first fortnight was spent with Michael; he was an experienced traffic officer. We spent a great deal of time on the motorway, which was something completely new to me, there were plenty of small traffic offences that I could deal with competently, which helped me decide that I did not want to work in the Traffic Department. During my last week with Michael, we were asked to work overtime in the Chesham area, this meant working until 2 am, which did not prove a problem. I thought we were going to patrol the streets of Chesham, but Michael had other ideas, he had been invited to a party in the town, we decided to attend that, which involved me drinking, my partner could not but he became very friendly with the hostess. It was time to leave and we returned to Amersham, once again overtime had been a drinking spree. Michael went missing for an hour during the party, then he appeared with the hostess, I was certain he had taken advantage of the situation, as well as the hostess.

My second fortnight on traffic was with Paul, he was also an experienced officer. We did a stint on the motorway, but that was nothing in comparison to what we got involved in later. I have seen Paul recently, he remembers the incident, but could not remember who was in the car with him, I must have made quite an impression. The incident occurred in Gerrards Cross, we were parked up listening to the radio, then we heard that a jeweller in our locality had been robbed, someone had taken down the registration of the vehicle, along with a description. We started to look out for the vehicle, hoping it would come our way, then it suddenly appeared in a line of traffic, we pulled out next to it but a bit further back. As we pulled up beside Paul suggested I jump out and grab the keys from the ignition, I stealthily got out of the car and moved towards the other vehicle, before I got close the driver saw me and the car speeded away from the roundabout. I got back into the car and Paul gave chase, I passed the details of the other car over the radio, along with which road we were on and our direction of travel, the radio was quiet as I spoke, other cars were listening in to see if they could assist. I looked at the car we were chasing, passing over descriptions of the three people on board, then the car changed lanes, he went to the opposite carriageway, which was in fact a dual carriageway heading towards us. We continued on the wrong side of the road for several miles, before hitting an area of London I did not know. Paul suggested I check the local railway station, to see if the three offenders were there, I got out of the car and went onto the platform, there was only an elderly lady waiting. I asked her if three men had come onto the platform, she was unable to help. I then left the station to return to the car, but the car had gone, a Met car turned up and told me to get in, they asked me about the robbers, my description seemed to please them. They said they thought they knew who they were, their local knowledge was incredible, but very pleasing, as we headed off to an address in a block of flats. One of the officers knocked on the door, a lady answered who knew the officers. They asked her where her son was, she was happy to tell us, along with who he was with, the officers were happy with the result. They believed, and rightly so, that they had two of the thieves, it was a waiting game, they would go back to the address later. I got back into the Met car and decided to scour the streets for our men, but we had no luck, but someone had found a tray of rings in the street, we went to the address. The tray of rings was handed to me, because the crime was committed in our area. You never realise that there are a lot of honest people in society, in the police we only deal with the rubbish. I eventually joined up with Paul, I thanked my Met colleagues for picking me up and showing me how quickly they were on the case.

The following morning, Paul and I were on early turn, but I was called down to the custody suite, where I was told that the Met had arrested the three men, I liked to think my description helped. All three men pleaded guilty at court, their previous convictions meant they would be spending some time at Her Majesty's pleasure, I cannot remember exactly what they got, but it was a long stretch. I remember that during the chase Paul's driving was superb, he even passed his father during the chase, he was at the side of the road as we went by, little did he know his son was driving. Paul tried to convince him he was the driver, I think he came around to the idea eventually, having never seen Paul drive in such a manner, I suppose it was not easy to accept. There was obviously more than the one chase, but the rest pails into insignificance after the chase.

There was another part of the job which did not really interest the officers taking part, but we all thought it was necessary.

At Little Chalfont there were public toilets in a car park, very close to a scout hut, where young boys met in the evening for their scouting activities, we all felt these young boys should be protected from certain persons who frequented the male toilets. I do believe these toilets were mentioned in a gay magazine as being a good place to meet other men, but I cannot be sure of that fact, but it was certainly advertised somewhere, although the people who went there were fairly local. The strange thing about these toilets, they were visited by ordinary guys, most of them were married, but they were still looking for sex with other men. Although they were not classed as gay men because of their marital status, I believe they were.

Let me first explain what we did. There were two cubicles in the male toilet, there was a large hole in the wall between the cubicles, I will leave it to your imagination to work out why the hole was there, it is not too difficult. We had been in touch with the local council, they had received complaints about these toilets, so it was time for us to act, and act as we did. They had given us the key to a pathway between the male and female toilets, that was where the ladder was kept, which we used to get onto the roof, where there was a skylight into the male toilets. It was decided to position two officers on the roof with a torch, this normally took place in the early evening, and two more officers in a plain car in the car park. If something happened that constituted an act of Gross Indecency, the torch was shone, then the officers in the car would enter the toilets, arresting those involved. Although the officer in the car made the arrest, the evidence was to come from those on the roof. This was not a pleasant job, but we felt children had to be protected, it was also hoped that these observations might frighten the men away, but that did not happen. We arrested and charged ten men, they all elected trial at the Crown Court, hoping the jury might be the type of men they were, this gave them a chance of getting off.

On one occasion, following the arrest of both men in the toilets, we went and searched their cars, this caused something of a surprise. In one car we found the uniform of a Salvation Army captain, the man admitted it was his uniform, so we checked on his occupation, I cannot remember what the result was. The circumstances were reported to the Salvation Army, I have no idea how they looked upon the incident.

On another occasion a Police Doctor was arrested, this required a report to the Chief Constable, he could not remain in that position, he was subsequently sacked.

The trials went as expected, the offenders being found guilty, but one trial still niggles me, I will explain it to you and you can decide.

I arrested one of two men in a compromising position in the toilets, both men were normally kept separate. When we arrived at the station I took my man to an interview room, he admitted the offence, he had previous convictions for it, I did not feel he was going to be a problem, I expected him to plead guilty at Magistrates Court. I never kept a close check on the case, I was surprised to receive a Crown Court warning for this particular case. I think I realised the other man arrested had something to do with the case going to the Crown Court, why or how I did not know. My suspicions were intensified when we got to the Crown Court. We were waiting in the designated room for police officers giving evidence, when a clerk for the prosecuting solicitor came into the room, he said the barrister was not proceeding with the case, which confused us all. Our Sergeant asked the clerk to bring down the solicitor, he left and returned a few minutes later, stating the solicitor had left the court, obviously afraid to meet his accusers. I knew at that point there was something not quite right, somebody had used whatever influence they had to stop the case, I suspected it was one of the offenders, the one I did not arrest. The Sergeant said he would put a report in about the proceedings, but that was not taken notice of. A few weeks later I was told I had to go to headquarters, the Assistant Chief Constable wanted to see me, I had no idea what it was about, but several of my colleagues on the Gross Indecency case had visited this gentleman, it was obviously to do with the case, I hoped it was good news. I arrived in plenty of time for my appointment, but I was kept waiting outside his office, I hoped he was apologising for the shoddy trial we had just witnessed. When I did go in I was surprised that this interview took place, the ACC told me I had been brought here to be offered advice, I questioned that, wanting to know why I was being offered advice. To my surprise, he said it was because he said he would do that, why I was being offered advice is still a mystery to this day. He also said that one of the defendants said I was not there at the time of his arrest. I agreed with him, which surprised him, if you consider that I had arrested his partner in crime, at least now I knew where all the trouble was coming from. The man I did not arrest had a lot of influence, enough to call off a trial, and enough for an ACC, a senior position, that the officers who carried out the arrests were not even there. I will not mention this ACC's name, although I should, for being bent, that is the only way I can describe him. He allowed a trial to be hijacked, then he had the cheek to offer advice to officers for doing their job, he was someone who had no backbone, he should never have been promoted to the rank of his incompetence. If he reads this book he will know who I am talking about, no doubt retired officers will know him as well. It saddens me that Senior Officers should be given such power, which they abuse without a second thought. I often wonder who the defendant with all the power was, it is unlikely I will find out now. At the time of the interview, I was told to leave, mainly because I complained about the way the trial was dealt with, he was unaccustomed to people answering back, if there was more of it he might not have had the power he did. I think he is retired now, I hope he enjoys the pension he did not earn. So, two men who committed the act of Gross Indecency were not only let off, but the officers dealing with the case were called liars by Senior Officers, thank goodness I am retired.

We had a problem in Chesham with travellers, that is the polite way to name them, gypsies was the general name, they were a bit of a problem. Most of them had the surname Smith, this was a surname they used so they could not be identified. Their ages varied as well, an adult would say he was fourteen, thinking that would prevent him being prosecuted, it did not mainly because we had a gypsy officer, that was his actual title, even though it was not politically correct. Whenever a traveller was stopped in the town, the first thing we did was get their name, then we called up our colleague, he would either verify the name, or in most cases tell the traveller to give the right details. He proved useful in other ways, the travellers had their own language, little did they know our officer understood the language, he often sat in on interviews. I remember stopping a truck with a driver on board, he said he was called John Smith, I called up my colleague, he turned up immediately. He looked at the traveller, then he checked the name he had given me.

"Elvis, you tell the officer your correct details," he said.

I was more likely to believe the name he had given me, instead he was called Elvis. I often wonder what parents are thinking of when they name their children, in the case of Elvis it is fairly obvious.

When we left Chesham we had a party, there is a picture to show that evening. There were many parties at Chesham, they normally took place in the single quarters. Many single women turned up at these parties, they knew these women in the single quarters, they were sort of groupies.

One of these officers was someone I knew quite well, when he told me that story of the night, I had no difficulty in believing what he said. He was someone who was unable to refuse any female who wanted sex with him, I think that was the case with this particular incident, she was well known to us, so this did not surprise us. He took her to his room, not wishing to make a spectacle of himself, they both stripped off ready for action, she laid in a provocative manner on the bed, across the bed rather than lengthwise. My friend tried unsuccessfully to have sex with her, but he did not have enough room to successfully complete the act. Once he had started to get his wicked way, my friend moved backwards and sat on the radiator, he moved off that very quickly, the radiator was red hot, it left him with burn marks which he was happy to show everyone.

We had a new recruit on our shift who we nicknamed Neo, because it was thought he looked like a Neolithic Man, not that any of us knew what such a person looked like, but the nickname stuck. He had dark very short hair, his complexion was dark. Unfortunately, he did not prove to be the brightest of human beings. On one particular night he turned up in a car to an emergency call from another officer, I along with a colleague had already turned up and arrested the offender. Whilst I was on the ground handcuffing this individual, a car turned up a screeched to a halt, Neo got out of the passenger side in shirt sleeves with braces, he had his helmet on, in his right hand was his truncheon. The prisoner I had handcuffed laughed out loud, I could not blame him for that.

Neo came to notice to a greater degree, as the tale I am about to tell you will show. We had arrived for a night shift at Chesham, it was just before 10 pm. Then came a call of a burglary in progress at a clothes shop in Amersham, we went to the cars and made our way a couple of miles up the road. As we approached the shop I saw a young man coming out of the shop door with trousers draped across his outstretched arms, it was not something I expected to see. The man did not drop the clothes, even though the police were approaching, he was arrested as his associate ran out the door, disappearing into the undergrowth. The grass was about two to three foot high, we knew he was in there somewhere, when suddenly there was a cry from a CID officer, who had arrived to help, maybe it was to get the arrest. The other man was arrested by CID, in fact, it was by the officer who had fallen over him. I saw the CID officer's statement when I was putting the file together, he said he had run after the suspect and detained him, that did sound better than falling over him, he was arrested which was the main thing. Both the offenders were interviewed about the burglary, what they said was something of a revelation. Both offenders knew Neo, in fact, they drank with him in the local pub, they had carried out the burglary because of what Neo had told them, no doubt in a drunken stupor. Neo told them that shifts change over at quarter to the hour, the 2 until 10 shift would be in the station when the night shift was being briefed, so nobody would be out on the streets, this was the best time to commit a burglary. It probably would have been if you got out of the shop quickly, but when you linger like our burglars did, there is a good chance of being caught, Neo did not explain that to his friends. The next question was how far did Neo's involvement go, he was interviewed about the matter, he admitted saying something to that effect, but he did not expect his friends to commit a burglary. Neo's friends had the same mental age as Neo, they did not run for when the alarm sounded, it was either stupidity or deafness, it is difficult to judge but I think I know the answer. After his initial interview by CID, Neo was interviewed by the Police Complaints Department, what he had done was not acceptable as a Police Officer, I think he started to appreciate that, but it took him a long time. Following the interview Neo was dismissed from the Force, it was the only action open to the Complaints Department. I am sure he did not receive any further punishment for the burglary, I think the board believed he was just stupid. His two friends were charged with burglary, they had a lot of previous convictions, they both received custodial sentences, Neo was lucky he did not receive the same. I never saw him after his interview, he was whisked away to headquarters to receive his marching orders.

There was another strange burglary in our area, at Little Chalfont to be exact, it took place in a block of flats, the people who lived in the flats were far from rich, most of the areas poor people lived there. To her credit the lady who lived in the burgled house had been doing a bit of spring cleaning in the house, this included a bit of painting. At the time of the burglary CID found a fingerprint in a piece of wet paint, it was checked out and a suspect was found. There was a question that the lady needed to be asked, had the gentleman next door been in her house when she was painting, she stated he had never been in her house, we had a surprise for her, it was her next-door neighbour's fingerprint. The man next door was at home when the police arrived, he was arrested and taken into custody, he admitted the offence, stating that he did not take anything, mainly because there was nothing of any value. It never ceased to amaze me how stupid some of these criminals are, he must have known he had put his finger in wet paint. It was the only time in my career that I was aware of someone committing a burglary, but not actually stealing anything. It was also the only time I came across a burglar leaving his calling card, leaving his fingerprint in wet paint.

I do remember on my first day at Chesham I got four hours overtime, I volunteered to take a prisoner to Oxford Prison, it was a new experience with overtime. The prisoner had just been remanded in custody by the Magistrates Court, the person we were taking was someone I would deal with during my career, a persistent thief, do not think he ever had a job. There are many people like that, a day's work is the last thing on their mind. These prison escorts became a good source of overtime, it was usually three to four hours overtime. We always handcuffed prisoners going to prison, a lot of the time they were handcuffed to an officer, I was not aware of anyone escaping while in police custody, but that was to be expected. There was paperwork to take, this had come from the court, prisons would not accept prisoners without a court warrant, which you can understand. Once the paperwork was completed inside the prison, at their reception area, we were free to leave, without the prisoner of course. Once outside in the courtyard the abuse from other prisoners started, it was verbal abuse only, I think they believed it upset us, it had the opposite effect. I wondered if they considered we were free, they were locked in a cell. I appreciate that to many of them it was the life they chose, three meals a day, a bed to sleep in, and no need to find a job. We drove off, leaving the prisoners to consider their wasteful actions, not that they thought they had anything to consider, their verbal abuses no doubt made them feel better. These prison escorts took place every week, now I believe there is a company that does the transportation, from the courts and to the courts, it is a lucrative business for that firm. I say that because the criminal fraternity will continue in their ventures, and the prisons will remain full. I enjoyed the prison escorts merely for the overtime, I had no wish to spend time with thieves and the like. There were officers who never volunteered for prison escorts, they obviously had no need for extra money, an interesting position to be in, but it left more overtime for the rest of us.

Two

Having moved to Amersham, there was a climatisation process we had to go through. The station was about ten times larger than Chesham, a lot more modern as I have already stated, there was even a shower in the changing rooms. On the top floor was a bar, which opened most nights, providing they had someone to work there, I am not aware of any payment for doing this job.

During that first couple of weeks, it was interesting to start the shifts at a new station, although it was not new to me, I had worked in the front office on many occasions. The station was open 24 hours a day, but the only people in the station after office hours were the Station Duty Officer and the civilian telephonist. Once we moved to Amersham it all changed, the whole shift was in during meal breaks.

On one of my first shifts at the station, I was allocated the Amersham car with a Woman Special Constable, it was our job to patrol the Amersham area in a marked Police car. No sooner had we got out of the station when we were sent to a fight in a car park of a local pub, there was a suggestion that ten men were involved. We were the first on the scene, I parked the car, both myself and the WPC approached the fight, those fighting looked up and the fight suddenly stopped. I asked all those there if anyone wished to make a complaint, nobody wished to, they all wanted to get home. I was a bit confused as to why nobody wanted to make a complaint, then I realised it. The lady I was with was not the most beautiful of creatures, in fact, she fitted the category at the bottom of the beauty stakes. It was not Halloween, but I seriously believe she frightened those fighting, even those watching started to move away, it was a very strange experience. It was not something I could mention to her, but I believe she was a good crime fighter, just by being there, an amazing crime prevention asset. I mentioned it to other officers, they did not believe it, but I was there, I saw it for myself.

While at Amersham I decided to spread my wings a little, I applied to attend a Plan Drawing course, which I was accepted for. The course lasted three weeks at Sulhamstead, that was the place we went when we initially joined. I was looking forward to it, I had an interest in Technical Drawing at school, this was a bit more important than that, it required the drawing of plans for serious offences. The plans were to be used in court, mostly to assist the jury, it was an important course, which I treated in such a way. There was another officer from Amersham on the course, he was a traffic officer, I remember he was a very good Plan Drawer, much better than I was. Being in traffic he did not carry out many of the drawings, that was where I came into my own, all the drawings that they wanted fell on my shoulders, but I needed someone to assist me. It was impossible to be at both ends of the tape at the same time, so Driver Handyman Keith assisted me. The first plan was for a murder in High Wycombe, it required several plans because of what happened at the scene. The victim was stabbed in the garage, he got away and crossed the road to the Royal British Legion building, but nobody was there, he then crossed the road again and ended up outside a doctor's surgery, but again there was nobody there. I believe this took place in the early evening, that was the reason the doctor was not there, but I thought there would have been someone at the British Legion, but that was not so. Why nobody helped him at the garage I did not know, I never received details of the offence, other than what was required for the court case, which was a shame as I might have been interested in the sequence of events. The good thing was that the offender had been arrested, but it begs the question when was he arrested, could nothing be done for the victim, or had he already died then. I actually did four plans for this case, one of the garage, one of the British Legion hall, one of the Doctor's surgery, and a plan combining all three locations. I think I had carried out a good plan or should I say plans. The case went to court and I was not called, but the offender was found guilty and sentenced to life imprisonment. Many years later my daughter mentioned she had gone to school with the murderer, I think he was in her class, little did he know what his future held for him, a very long sentence.

To carry out my plans a small room was set aside for me, it had a drawing board and all the instruments I was likely to need to complete an acceptable drawing.

On each occasion, except for the first one, I got a Crown Court warning, which I did not mind, it gave me the opportunity to explain my drawing to the jury.

There was a serious assault at a wine bar in Amersham, I constructed a drawing as was required by me, it was a good effort, and I received my court warning. I went to court and explained my plan to the jury, who I believe understood it. I was not convinced my evidence helped the case, but the defendant was found guilty, he was sentenced a few weeks later, what that was I do not know, I had carried out my bit.

We had a series of burglaries in Amersham, not that usual you might think, and of course, you would be right, except these burglaries had a twist. One of the burglars was described as black, once again not something that brought the house down, but in Amersham it was, there was only one black person in the town, and he had ginger hair, but the hair colour was not recognised by the witnesses. We looked around the town to find our pair of burglars, then we saw them walking down the driveway of a house, we got out of the car to question them, then the inevitable line arrived.

"You only stopped us because I'm black," said the black man.

For the first time in my career, I said the words which confused him.

"That's right, that is exactly why I stopped you," I said.

The man looked confused, no Police Officer had ever said that to him before, he did not know what to say, so he said nothing. At the same time CID turned up, we allowed them to take the prisoners away, a mistake I was to later find out. We went to the back of the property and found a broken window, but our burglars were disturbed by a neighbour, she heard the breaking glass, she was about to telephone the police when we turned up.

We then went to custody to interview our prisoners, the Custody Sergeant asked if we had arrested the two men, we said we had, then he showed us the information on the charge sheet, the CID men had put their names down as arresting officers. He immediately crossed their names out, replacing them with our names, this sometimes happened at Amersham when the CID men were short of work, it made you aware of offers made by CID. I do believe the custody sergeant spoke to the CID officers concerned, all they were doing was trying hard to impress their superiors, showing how many arrests they made. Both the men pleaded guilty at court, CID were not asked to attend the hearing.

There was a strange series of events that took place at Amersham, it involved one of the officers, he had decided to have an affair with a lady from a block of flats just outside the main town, not exactly a desirable area to live. Our colleague was not too worried about what anybody thought, he was only after one thing. Perhaps I should mention there was a lady waiting for him at home, she knew nothing of the affair, she was probably the only one in the station who did not know, which always appears to be the case, she was also a serving Police Officer. Although they were not married, she classed it as a serious relationship. They worked the same shift pattern, but he was on a different beat, he worked in Chesham, she worked in Amersham. I am unsure if he met his lady friend on a regular basis, or if he met her during work time. The affair never came to light with CID on the station, this was to happen later. CID was aware that drug dealers frequented these flats, so they decided to plan a raid, confident that drugs would be found, so it came to pass. Unfortunately, the whole station was aware of the raid, including lover boy, that was where things got a little messy, the raid was carried out as planned, no drugs were found in the flats CID targetted. How did the dealers get to know about the raids there was only one person who could tip them off, although this could not be proved he was the snitch, all for sex, his intervention never came to light, uniform officers knew but said nothing. Perhaps he should have faced up to his accusers, but it never happened. It appears he knew of the raids and passed it to his lady friend, she told the dealers, the flats were cleaner than they had ever been. Two further strange aspects of the story, the first was that the girlfriend never knew he was giving out the information, CID had no idea either, which does not surprise me. In circumstances like this the girlfriend is always the last to know, I am not sure if she ever knew the true facts. Yet another strange fact from this case, our grass applied to join CID, he passed the board, he was transferred to Milton Keynes, he certainly had someone looking after him. He should have been thrown out, not rewarded for what he did. I have no idea how many man-hours were wasted planning these operations, like everyone in the station something should have been said, but the word informing springs to mind, but he really should have been informed on. Another aspect was he was very friendly with a Chief Inspector at the station, a man nobody liked very much, maybe that helped him through his CID board, I do not know how. His transfer to Milton Keynes brought up another story, which I will relay to you now.

Although he was stationed on CID at Milton Keynes, he lived in Aylesbury, coming home each night to his devoted girlfriend, but things were about to change drastically. His girlfriend was at home when there was a knock on the door, there she was confronted by a young lady carrying a black sack, which emptied in the hallway, nothing was said at that time. Words similar to these were said.

"Tell him it is all over, this is his clothes, I never want to see him again."

The girlfriend was a little taken aback, she did not know her boyfriend was seeing someone at Milton Keynes, but then she knew nothing of the affair at Little Chalfont, but all this overtime he was doing started to make sense. She waited patiently for her boyfriend to return home, perhaps the term ex-boyfriend might seem appropriate, when he did, an argument ensued, followed by him being kicked out on the streets. Where he slept that night is unknown, but I feel there was another girlfriend waiting somewhere, people like him got away with all the misdemeanours they encounter, but no doubt he was helped by the Chief Inspector, who I believe was also a womaniser. The man in question was later transferred to Greater Manchester, why they wanted him is beyond me, but no doubt the Chief Inspector put in a favourable report, I remember him on shift, particularly night shift, he told his girlfriend how many hours of sleep he had got. I travelled from Aylesbury with them, he was not what I would call hard-working, but he got away with it, mainly because he had a Chief Inspector in his corner.

I remember one night shift when we had to pick up a prisoner in London, Acton to be exact, we left at 4 am, when the streets were quiet. Two of us took a panda, expecting to be there and back in no time. We parked in the station car park in Acton, expecting to be in and out in a few minutes. We made our way to the custody suite, I was amazed to see the queue of prisoners to be booked in, but we were expected, our man was handed over immediately. I asked one of the officers what it was like earlier in the evening, he said it got really busy then. On leaving I thought if this was a quiet time, with a queue of prisoners to be booked in, I could not imagine what it was like earlier in the evening, particularly when the pubs kicked out. Being busy was always the best, it meant time went by quickly.

A surprising incident happened at Amersham, it was in the Police Station. A colleague of mine was on the front desk, a well dressed and well-groomed lady came into the station, she was in possession of a small bag, from that bag she pulled out a carving knife covered in blood. My colleague stepped back, not sure if her intention was to use it on him, thankfully it was not, she was merely admitting to a crime she had committed. She stated she had murdered her husband with the knife, she was apparently very calm, which was more than can be said for my colleague, but he acted in a professional manner. He told her to stay where she was, he moved the knife out of the way, they joined her in the foyer, there he arrested her on suspicion of murder. It is a shame he did not think about it, he should have called CID, they would have arrested her, but he would have been trampled in the rush. She was taken to the custody suite and booked in, her house keys were taken, the house was checked out, there was a dead body of a man in the house, he had several stab wounds. I know there is no particular kind of person who is capable of committing murder, but she was well dressed, attractive, unlike any murderer I have seen, not that I had seen many. I did not know the circumstances of the offence but she pleaded guilty at Crown Court, she was sentenced to Life Imprisonment. It was certainly a strange scenario, but in saying that it was probably more difficult to hide the murder from friends and family, it was not as if she had thought about, she could have broken a window and said it was a burglar, but she was too honest.

While I was at Amersham I was sent on a Police Driving Course at Banbury, it was a three-week course and I was looking forward to it, although my driving experience was somewhat limited, having only recently passed my driving test. I was glad to say the Driving Course would change my lack of experience, at least that was what I was hoping. The course took us to many places, there were three officers in each car with an instructor, this meant that each student drove for two hours each day, in that time we could travel a long way. One day we drove to Crewe, somewhere I had never been, there we had lunch, then we drove back to Banbury, it was a long day, but we all had plenty of driving. One of our crew was talking about his girlfriend, which was a mistake, but the subject continued, then we asked him why she went out with him, the reply surprised us all.

"Because I'm hung like a bison," he replied.

That confused us all, none of us had any idea if a bison was well endowed or not, he thought he was on to a winner, but the instructor thought differently.

The following day we made our way to Whipsnade Zoo, confident a bison would be on display, we asked a member of staff where the bison were located. She told us but looked very confused with our enquiry, I do not think she had ever been asked that question before. We did not feel it was necessary to explain why we wanted to see the bison, but I think she would have understood if we had told her. We found the bison eventually; it was a bit of a disappointment, particularly for our colleague who had initially brought up the subject.

During the course a member of the public complained about a particular piece of driving they had witnessed, all such complaints must be looked into, which this one was, to the satisfaction of the complainant. The incident was along a narrow road, the police car was seen travelling on the wrong side of the road as it approached a bend, it was a valid point under normal circumstances, but this was far from normal. It was explained that there was a police vehicle in front of the vehicle he had seen, this vehicle was passing instructions to the other vehicle, telling him the road ahead was clear, he could then cross into the other carriageway when going around bends, the gentleman accepted and appreciated the explanation.

During this course, we had a long trip to North Wales, where exactly we went I do not remember, but we travelled uphill in a mountainous region, with very windy roads. There were many other trips, mostly fairly local, it was a long time ago, it is difficult to recall them now, but I passed the course, that was the most important aspect of the course.

We had a new Superintendent at Amersham, who became quite a character, although I doubt he knew that, he was a nice man. He did have difficulty in remembering people's names, as the following will show. He saw a Sergeant in the corridor, he asked him if he knew a particular Sergeant, which he said he did, he then asked him to get the Sergeant to come and see him. The Sergeant agreed to carry out the task, which he was able to do quite easily. No doubt you have already guessed, he wanted to see the Sergeant he had just been speaking to, he went and saw the boss, but there was no mention that this was the

Sergeant he had spoken to. The Superintendent decided to put up a board in his office, it would contain photos of all the officers on the station, a wise move you might think, except for one fatal flaw, he left his office door open at night. It was typical of a policeman's obscure sense of humour, on the night shift the photos were changed around, nobody fitted his photo, it took a while to get the right photos back in the right place. The Superintendent's door was locked after that, a wise move. Our leader had problems with our annual reports, he kept mixing people up. On one occasion an officer was asked how his children were doing at school, which surprised him somewhat, he was not married and had no children, but it was passed off. It was then found out he was looking at the wrong file, he eventually got to the one he wanted, completing the appraisal with no more mishaps. Whenever I was asked to carry out a Plan Drawing, I needed the Superintendent's permission, for obvious reasons, it meant I had to be taken off the shift. On this particular occasion, he said we should check with the Chief Inspector, not the same Chief Inspector I had mentioned previously, this one was an efficient officer, with a good reputation. I cannot remember everything the Superintendent said, but hopefully, the following is a close facsimile.

"PC Rabbit has asked to do a Plan Drawing, will that be alright?" he said.

I looked at the Chief Inspector, I stood behind the Superintendent and watched the reaction, it was difficult for him not to smile, I already had a large smile on my face. The Chief Inspector said he thought it would be alright, then he smiled, the Superintendent left the office, we both laughed but not out loud. It was one of his mistakes, mixing up people's names, but where PC Rabbit came from still confuses me, I know I was sometimes called Bunny at school, that must have been the origin of the mix-up. Other people who saw him said he did not get their names right, they were sometimes confused by what he said. I have seen this gentleman since we both retired, he calls me by my first name on these occasions, I have never mentioned what he sometimes called me, but life is rarely straightforward.

There is someone that needs a particular mention, he was the judge at Aylesbury Crown Court, before he became a recorder in London, a man who criminals feared. Once again it would seem unfair to mention his name, although I believe he might have passed away. On a few occasions at court, the defendants have asked the Police who the presiding judge is on that day, when his name is mentioned their faces drop, not because he will treat them unfairly, quite the opposite. He sits in his chair and listens to the case, sometimes he looks like he has dropped off to sleep, but he misses nothing when he sums up all the details presented to the jury. The thing I liked about him was his summing up, he had a way of indicating to the jury what their verdict should be, he was a master of his trade, a judge all Police Officers liked.

I remember giving evidence in front of him, the defence solicitor asked me a question which he had already asked, that was when the judge jumped in, I remember exactly what he said.

"My officer has already answered that question, do not ask it again."

That was enough for the solicitor, he did not repeat the altercation with the judge.

Another aspect of life at Amersham concerned PSU training, this was a unit being trained using shields. One day a month we had our training day, it was at RAF Benson, the deserted part, we did not want the locals seeing police officers in riot gear, it would affect their security, so we were kept out of the way. Once on site the training began, it started with a one-mile run, not too strenuous you might think, but the strain was increased when you had to carry a four-foot shield, but not all carried the shields. There were some officers, those at the rear of the shield unit, they did not carry anything, but that changed over time. Those without shields carried a fire extinguisher on their backs, they might well have been heavier than the shields. Once the run was complete we were able to move onto the shield work, not that easy when you are dripping with sweat, but it had to be done, even if you felt uncomfortable. This run was carried out in our PSU suits, making it even hotter next to the skin. The shield work could not be carried out without a crowd, which was provided by another PSU from a different area of the Force. Their intention was to act as a hostile crowd, continually throwing wooden bricks at us. We did on one or two occasions use petrol bombs, the instructors explained how to overcome these missiles, and we dealt with them very well. I think we were the first, and possibly only Force, to use petrol bombs. After the morning session, we went to the Mess to be fed, I remembered how good the food was when I had been stationed at RAF Benson in my RAF days, the food was still good, except the appetite was that much bigger after a hard morning. When it was time to return to our stations we slumped onto the coaches exhausted, little did we know then that this training would be useful in 1984. On reaching our home station the staff were surprised at the state we had gotten into, leaking wet with sweat, not a pleasant sight, it put off some of the officers not on a PSU, but then they were not the type for such duties. There were officers who in 1984 when the PSU officers were earning good overtime, complained about it, but they had never volunteered to be on a PSU, now the jealousy crept in. These officers were not allowed to go, mainly because they had received no training, which to me seemed fair, I had worked hard on our PSU training days, as did all those on the PSU. I never minded the training, I was relatively fit, but some of the officers struggled, in most cases, it was those with a weight problem. This training did not help us when we went to Greenham Common, which was something of a problem, dealing with women who had nothing better to do with their lives than live in a tent, next to a gate, where cruise missiles were being brought in. They were not going to stop it, even though the missiles moved several years later, it had little to do with their protest, they made me think that it gave them something to hold onto. The duties carried out at Greenham Common were boring and time-consuming, but that will be discussed later, now back to PSU training. Although we trained once a month, we also acted as the crowd on several occasions, but we were not given wooden bricks as we thought, this was because many of the windows in the houses had been smashed. The houses were not being used to accommodate people, the area was used as a PSU training area. Instead of bricks, we were given bags of flour, which I feel was more expensive than the bricks, but someone had made the decision so flour it was, what happened when the overalls were washed intrigued me, but not for long. We did what we needed to do, throwing flour at the PSU as it advanced towards us. This PSU had an Inspector we did not like, I had a feeling his own troops had very little time for him. It might appear a bit juvenile, but the bags of flour were heading in his direction, even the shield he had could not protect him, he was white all over, he looked like a ghost. To his credit he did not complain, he must have noticed most of his officers were clean, he probably thought it was because of his rank, he was the only one who thought that. I do not recall ever seeing the inspector again, he was absent from all the Greenham Common events, and I do not recall him during the Miner's Dispute, perhaps he gave up his position on the PSU. Once the flour had run out we were back on wooden bricks, but most of them were thrown at the windows, it was a sort of competition with the crowd. Acting as the crowd was a good duty, it was not very tiring and we got well fed.

Returning back to the station, there were several events that need mentioning, mainly because these events do not happen anymore, but in these earlier years they happened frequently. They were called set-ups, it was something that happened to new recruits on the shift. It was usual for the whole shift to be involved, this included the sergeants, at least it did with my shift, I think it was common practice. Perhaps it is best to set up the scenario, then you can hopefully follow the plot. This involved another shift, one of the officers got on a wetsuit, he placed himself in the pond in the park, he also was wearing a blonde wig. A WPC on the shift was sent to the park to investigate the call received by the police station, stating there was a body in the pond. She rushed to the scene and saw the body, she stripped off down to her underwear and jumped in, the pond was not very deep, so she waded out to where the body was. When she got there she realised what had been going on, I think she nearly drowned the officer acting as the victim. As she got out she was photographed, but she was given the negatives. Also at the scene was the man I mentioned earlier, the one who was always out at night, I shudder to think what he thought of it, but he certainly never mentioned it. Many years later there was an incident at Milton Keynes, during one of these set-ups, after that, they were banned, but I have no idea what the incident was, no doubt someone was badly injured.

Another set-up involved me, but I must stress all these set-ups took place in the early hours of the morning when the town was quiet, it would have been impossible at any other time.

To return to this set-up for an officer on our shift, my involvement was possible because my duty was due to finish at 2 am, the rest of the shift was working until 6 am. Someone had got me a combat jacket, I also had a full face mask, long hair included, but of course, I had a radio so I knew what was going on. The first part was that John, he was the one to be set up, was out walking with another officer, then they received a call of someone behind a row of shops. I knew where they were so I stood at the end of the row of shops, about 50 yards away, waiting for them to appear, when they did I ran for it, I was picked up by a waiting panda car and driven off. I heard John on the radio, he said he had chased me but I had disappeared. The next sighting of me was in the park, once again off again I knew where they were, when John appeared I ran to the waiting car, quickly driving away. John called in again, stating I had disappeared again, he was starting to get frustrated, it was now time to end it. Another called up John saying he had arrested this person, could he come back to the station to identify him. I was placed in a cell facing the wall, John was brought into the cell and asked to identify me, which he said he could not do because of the mask I was wearing. Bearing in mind I had never taken the mask off it was a strange request, the sergeant then asked John why I had been arrested, he was happy to say it was being drunk and disorderly, which confused me as he had not been within 50 yards of me. I took the mask and John appreciated what had happened, he accepted it without question.

There were many other set-ups, but those are the only two I can remember with any clarity.

My next tale relates to a famous individual, I do not think I can mention his name, although I must because there is a picture in the book, I do not think he would mind. We were called to a house in Little Chalfont, a large house with security gates, lived in by Ozzy Osbourne and his wife Sharon. We received a telephone call from Sharon, stating that Ozzy was trying to kill her, we went to the address at great speed, having arrived at the house we realised we needed the code to get inside. Sharon gave us the code and we entered the grounds of the property, I remained outside as other officers went into the house. Ozzy was brought out by two officers, I think he was in handcuffs, he appeared to be under the influence, he was placed in the police car and brought to Amersham. There he was booked in and placed in a cell, it was hoped he would sleep until the morning, which I believe he did, then we had to take him to court.

The offence came under Beaconsfield Magistrates, so that was where he had to be taken. I got him a cup of tea which he thanked me for, he was a completely different person when he was sober, I spoke to him about the situation, but he said it was the drink, which I could well believe. He did say he was drinking a bottle of vodka a day, this obviously did not help his moods. He said why he had lost his temper with Sharon, but I am not going to discuss it in this book. I and a colleague were taking him to court, the picture shows us outside the court. There were a lot of photographers there, so I asked Ozzy if he wanted to go into court with a blanket over his head, he decided against that, saying it was good publicity. I suppose to anyone in that business, all publicity is good publicity.

He was eventually dealt with by the court, we left him in the hands of someone who was taking him to be cured, I cannot say any more than that, I have nothing more about him, apart from little bits on the television, maybe it worked, I hope so for his sake. I enjoyed talking to him, he was a pleasant man when sober.

In a Transit van outside Beaconsfield Magistrates Court with Ozzy Osbourne and PC Andy Martin

I believe the Osbournes have now moved from Little Chalfont, but maybe Ozzy is just being very quiet. I remember inside the house, I had a quick look, there was a recording studio, whether he produced any records there I do not know, why would I.

I also met Dave Lee Travis early one morning, he was returning from London. Another brief acquaintance was Noel Edmonds, I found him in an antique store, I tried to get him to start our local Half Marathon, but he was unable to help.

There was a situation which occurred in a public house in Chesham, they had a problem with a young man we all knew well, he was someone who disliked the police, at least that was the impression he gave to his small of hangers-on, there was no doubt he could be a handful, although I never witnessed that. The story was that he was an ex-professional boxer, I followed boxing but it was not a name I was familiar with. It leads to the question of how good this man was, who had apparently retired from the profession, which seemed a little strange, he was still a young man. He still looked in good shape so I did not want to question his credentials, but the three who hung around with him could tell you how good he was, it was called hero worship by these three, no doubt he built himself for their entertainment, which they were glad to consent to this illustrious career. I never found out if he was a boxer or not, but his fan club was sure of the facts, I think it was a certain amount of fear, keeping on his side helped their image. When he came out of the pub he saw us waiting, he told his men to hold him back, which they did as requested, it was his way of stopping himself from attacking us, I think it was for his followers more than us. He was one of those people who talks a good job, there were several in the police like that, whether he would attack the police or not is unknown, but I felt it was unlikely. I feel sure he prepared his minders before approaching the police, he had probably seen us through the pub window. On this night he was arrested by the most junior member of the shift, he did not make a big fuss, his minders stayed out of the way, there is no doubt he had briefed them to keep out of it. They always turned up at the police station when he was arrested, sitting in the foyer waiting for the return of their hero. Inside the station he conformed to all requests, it was when he left, he told his gang he had not done anything the police requested, which is what they wanted to hear. I am sure his life was great inside his head; he still had his loyal followers. I came across this gentleman on several occasions, he was never a real problem, but he was in his own mind, and of course in the mind of his followers. On the occasions I met him in the police station, he was always very polite and relatively friendly, it was when he met his minders, then he had to put on an act, a shame none of the police officers believed his act.

There was another character in Chesham that needs a special mention, he was an Indian gentleman who was built like an ox, his strength was added to by his lack of intelligence, although that is not completely true. He was far from that, he appeared that way because he lived in his own world, which was a complicated world, only he knew how this world worked. I remember him being arrested in Chesham, it took four CID officers to drag him to the station. The offence was relatively minor, but it had to be dealt with, my recollection was that it was a theft, but he had to be put before the court. He was taken to Amersham to spend the night in the cells before his appearance before the magistrates in the morning, his first of many requests did not take long, he wanted the Home Secretary to be informed of his arrest, we told him that would be done. A few hours later, around midnight, he asked if the Home Secretary had responded, we told him he was in bed but he would respond in the morning, he was content with that answer. He kept talking all through the night, little did I know this man was responsible for the Second World War, I had the misbelief it was Hitler, but he put me right on that. He was involved in the Kennedy assassination, as well as other wars, but I was now starting to get bored, so I told my sergeant, he had a plan. About 3 am we took him along the underground passage to the court, several members of the shift were allocated roles in the court, the case was heard, he was given a six-month sentence, which he appeared to accept. On his return to his cell he dropped off to sleep, nothing more was heard from him for the remainder of the night.

The following afternoon our shift was back on duty, I was sent to the custody suite, our Indian friend was still in his cell, he had not yet gone to court, I was to take him when the time came. I was sure he would not remember what had happened the previous night, how mistaken could I have been. I took him to court, which caused him a little confusion, he stood before the magistrates and the theft charge was read out, he was asked how he pleaded.

He then went on at length to explain that he had already been dealt with for this offence, the magistrates asked him when it had been dealt with, he said last night. The magistrates looked at me and I shrugged my shoulders, this appeared to indicate to them that this man was not all there. They played along with his mind games and found him guilty, sentencing him to 3 months, which pleased him, he decided to share that with the court, it was less than I got last night. The magistrates shook their heads as he left the court. This was the last time I had any contact with this man, I do not know if he still frequents the Chesham area.

One further incident I believe you might find interesting, before I move onto Greenham Common, Hungerford and other events. I was on foot patrol in Amersham town centre, it was very quiet, then a group of youths passed me, they had obviously just left the pub. They walked up the road without speaking, but I took no notice of that. When they had reached the top of the road, about 50 yards away, there was an almighty crash, which I went to investigate, one of these eight youths had decided to kick off the litter bin. It was in the street, damaged beyond repair, I politely asked who had done it, there was no reply, I then told all eight of them they were under arrest for causing criminal damage, then I called for the transit van. They thought it amusing that one officer could arrest eight men, when the transit arrived the smiles were wiped from their faces. The driver was our sergeant, a very large rugby player, he encouraged each of them to get into the transit. They were taken to Amersham and booked in, they all refused to talk to me, then it was time to look into their backgrounds, which proved very interesting. One of the group was training to be a solicitor, another had his sights set on being an architect, these were going to be the first two people I interviewed. I asked the architect if someone would employ him if he had a criminal record, he had not considered that. I explained that if the culprit was not found, all of them could be charged with criminal damage, giving them a criminal record, I think the message got through. He told me who the offender was, but I needed confirmation from the solicitor, he was brought out next, I told him the same as the architect. He was quick to give me the name, it was the same name. Seven of them were released, they were lectured by the sergeant, they knew what they had done was wrong, wasting police time amongst other things. It is very strange that grassing on someone is not good, unless your career is in jeopardy.

Just one more story before we move on, you may even find this one amusing. I was parked up with a colleague in Amersham Old Town, Tesco's car park, directly across the road from a bus stop, there was a man in the bus stop. It was early in the morning so he was not waiting for a bus, but he was someone we knew, a person who has been known to cause damage, he needed no reason to do this. We decided to watch him as there was nothing else happening, the town had been checked and it was quiet. Suddenly, without any warning, the man decided to smash the glass, he brought out something from his pocket. I started the car to go to the bus stop, but I stopped in my tracks, another police pulled up in front of the bus stop, the man was bundled into the car and driven off. There is a moral in this story, but I have no idea what it is.

Three

Greenham Common and Hungerford

This chapter will talk about the above subjects, along with others you may find interesting.

Within Thames Valley our biggest commitment appeared to be Greenham Common, this went on for several years and was not particularly liked by officers. On each occasion we were required a telex was sent from force Headquarters, stating that we were going to an unknown destination, after the first one the wording should have changed, particularly if I location was meant to be secret. When the telex came in stating the unknown destination, everyone knew where we were going, it became something of a joke, at least this way our families could be told where we were going.

Greenham Common at the time was overrun with women, I am pretty certain there were no men there, they were protesting about nuclear weapons, in the form of cruise missiles, being stored on British soil. The missiles had arrived from the United States, the British government had come to some sort of agreement with the Americans, what that was only the government knew, and it was unlikely they were going to tell us. The protesters appeared to have a good system in preparation for the missiles, there were protesters on the route who relayed messages back to Greenham, but this did not work too well in the middle of the night, normally when the missiles arrived. I had no idea how they were shipped into Britain, but during the day the women were ready for the arrival of the missiles, at night they rarely made it out of their tents. We sometimes stood at empty gates as the missiles arrived, and the missiles were very long, I estimate between 20 and 30 foot long, I have no idea what damage it caused.

The camp itself was set up in September 1981, after a group of Welsh women arrived at Greenham to protest. They realised that their march there was not going to get them the attention that was needed to get rid of the missiles. After that women started to stay on the site, they were able to blockade the site. The first blockade took place in March 1982, there were 250 women protesting, during this there were 34 arrests, a small amount in comparison to what was to come. The first act of resistance came in September 1981, 36 women chained themselves to the base of the fence. On the 29th September 1982, the women were evicted from the site by Newbury District Council, but a new camp was set up within days. In December 1982 over 30,000 women turned up on the site, they joined hands around the base. Where these women came from is a mystery, they certainly came from outside the Thames Valley area, it is possible they came from all over the country. Maybe they did not know what to do as Christmas was approaching, they decided to treat themselves to a trip to wonderful Berkshire.

The camp became very well known on 1st April 1983, when 70,000 protesters formed a fourteen-mile human chain from Greenham to Aldermaston, on their way to the ordnance factory at Burghfield, quite an undertaking, hopefully, this time they proved their point, whatever it was.

On the 4th April 1984, the women were again evicted from the site, surely the District Council were wasting their time, it did not work on the last occasion, why did they think it would work this time. To everyone's surprise by nightfall many of the women had returned to reform the camp, why do these councils not learn a lesson, I appreciate they do not move the women, that is left to someone else to do, they sit in their offices and do the paperwork. In 1987 Parliament were told there were no more protesters there, but small groups of protesters cut into the fence on the perimeter, I wonder if they told Parliament that, I doubt it. The protesters were in nine groups around the site, at different locations, most of them were at different gates, a sensible move on their part.

The last missile left the base in 1991, but the camp remained there until 2000, the obvious question was why, perhaps they had been there so long, they did not have a home to go back to. I cannot see any logical reason for remaining there for nine years, unless someone told them the missiles were coming back, that is an interesting theory, perhaps it should be looked into.

On my first visit there I saw the missiles at first hand, as previously mentioned, they were certainly a frightening sight, I had never seen one before. We lined either side of the gate, leaving enough room for the transporter to pass unhindered, our main objective was to make sure the women never stepped into the road, the transporters were told not to stop. In all the times I visited the site, none of the women stepped into the road, maybe they had been told the vehicles would not stop, that must have been the reason. We usually only spent one night there, that was when the missiles were coming in. During the winter of one year, I cannot remember exactly when, we were to spend a week of nights on the perimeter fence, walking around it, it was a security exercise. The women had threatened to break into the base, we were checking they did not do that. I think it was February, I know it was bitterly cold. During the day the Metropolitan Police had been on our stretch of land, they had pulled down and uprooted trees, they used the wood in the 45-gallon drums that were around the outside, mainly to keep themselves warm. Where we were the Met had built a small enclosed hut type of erection, it only had room for two people, we took in turns resting in this hut, it was a very good construction. We went to the nearby wood and brought back wood for the fire, which we built inside the 45-gallon drum, once it got started it blazed away, we crowded around it until it was time to go on patrol. The man in charge of the operation was an ACC, not the same as before but he had the ACC's mentality. He decided there were to be no fires on the perimeter, he would check out the perimeter during the night, this he did by using the force helicopter, I bet you thought he was going to walk along the perimeter. When you consider the force had either three or four ACC's, I had come across two of them, but appeared to be a waste of time, their wages could have been spent on equipment the officers needed. We had the fire blazing when the helicopter went over, he was bound to see it from his warm cockpit, which of course he did, he requested the officer in charge of that part of the perimeter should go and see him, our inspector made his way to Ascot racecourse to confront the ACC, which he was more than capable of doing. On his return he told us the ACC was comfortable in his office at the racecourse, the central heating was on so he was nice and warm. Our fire remained burning, I do not think the ACC took to the air again, maybe our inspector had told him a few home truths, which would not have surprised us. He invited the ACC to join us on the fence, particularly if he thought it was too warm for fires, he refused the inspectors offer, which did not surprise us. The whole week was a disaster, we never saw any of the women, perhaps our fence was not to their liking, but wait we did.

Our shift for this event started at 6 pm, we would remain until 6 am, it was a twelve-hour night shift, which provided us with one good situation, we were earning four hours overtime each night. When we completed our night shift another force took over from us, we were relieved by the Met, they had brought their axes with them, it was obvious what they intended to do. I wondered whether they had the equivalent to an ACC spying on them, I suspected not, the fire was started as soon as they arrived, they were well organised, it had snowed during the night making it that much colder.

Greenham was an interesting place for amusing stories, usually relating to the officers working there. One morning, when we had turned up at the secret location, the missiles were about to be brought in, the women were waiting, which as I have said was not always the case, but on this early morning, they hung around the gate. Although I was never sure I suspected the missiles were brought into RAF Brize Norton, it was a large station that could cope with the long missile. Wherever it was the women knew when the missiles were en route, they had spies on the way, they informed those at the gate where the missiles were and how long before they reached Greenham. I did ask one of the women how far away were the missiles, she looked at me with disgust, refusing to pass on this information to the enemy, that was how they classed the police. I bet they would have been on the phone if something had been stolen from their tent, it is a strange scenario the world over, lose something, or get broken into, the police are called, for all other cases, the police are the enemy.

On one of our early morning visits to the base, we made our way to the main gate, it was a filthy night, it had been raining non-stop. The sergeant told us to prepare to alight, one of our team was very keen to get out, he opened the door and stood by it waiting for the signal. As we stopped we were told to get out, the enthusiastic officer was first out, he had hoped to land on solid, instead, he went right into a ditch full of water, I would estimate it was about three foot deep, it had rained a lot that night. Although he wanted to get out of the ditch, he was unable to do so, there was nobody there to help him, we were still in the transit laughing at our unfortunate colleague. Fortunately, this was one of those nights when the women had a lay in, they never witnessed the incident, we helped our colleague out of the ditch, he was put in the transit. When the women were up and about they stood right in front of you, sometimes they spoke to us, asking if we knew there were missiles coming into the base, of course, we did, that was the reason for us being there. I think this was planned in the hope it would wind up the officers, but we were too well trained to listen to women who lived at the side of the road. I was on occasions tempted to enter into a conversation with them, asking them if their husbands minded them living where they did, and in many cases smelling like they did, there were no washing facilities there, when they got close they did smell bad. It is strange that their opinion was the only one, they stated that these missiles were going to cause a world war, which they were, providing they were used. At that time they acted as a deterrent, the Russians knew they were there, but they were not going to act, knowing these missiles could be launched on their cities, it was a game of cat and mouse. I never thought nuclear missiles would ever be used, I had seen these missiles in my RAF days when I worked on the V force, but the women at Greenham knew more than I did. I often wondered where their information came from, probably a comment on the internet. To return to Greenham Common, the women had put themselves in front of the gates, they were asleep when we arrived, but they had to be moved. Our sergeant, who was a shrewd officer said they must be asked to leave, if they did not leave then they could be arrested. He spoke in a low voice asking them to leave, the women remained asleep, he told the officers to remove the women, in total 18 women were arrested that morning, and the gate was clear. It was used on a few occasions, it worked every time, many because the women were asleep, they all stated they had never heard them being asked to move, neither did I and was stood near the sergeant. I cannot remember how long Greenham Common went on, to me it was a complete waste of time, but what do I know, I never had the internet at that time.

Greenham Common Woemen's Peace Camp.

Our PSU training was used on two further occasions, both were away from the force area, the first was at Handsworth in the West Midlands, we were sent for because of riotting in the city, at last we might be able to use the training we had been given. This riot happened on the 10th July 1981, we went there looking forward to quelling a riot. We went into Handsworth Police station and waited, we were fed and watered but no call came. We were sent home in the early afternoon, the rioting had been sorted out.

A second riot, which would prove more serious, took place four years later, it was in Toxteth in Liverpool, once again we waited but saw no action, returning home again.

Another riot that happened was much closer to home, near to High Wycombe there was some trouble, but not enough to concern us. The Chief Inspector in charge gave us an informal chat, knowing we had our riot gear and shields, he emphasised that no riot gear or shields were going to be used, he hoped the situation would fizzle out. The situation did not get any worse, we stood there and controlled everything that had happened. We had not seen the Chief Inspector for a while, then he reappeared in full riot gear carrying a short shield, it was quite unbelievable, he did not appear to be too embarrassed. A short while later the mini riot subsided, but the Chief Inspector remained in his riot gear, we left and went back to Amersham, but you can imagine who was the topic of the conversation. I now had two ACC's and one Chief Inspector who were complete morons, I really am glad that I have retired. The Chief Inspector was a wonderful human being, he thought of himself first, the rest of us meant nothing to him, I do not think he had the respect of anyone after this incident.

The PSU came into action when we searched for Malcolm Fairley, this was in the summer of 1984. Fairley became known as the Fox, he was prevalent in three towns below the Chilterns, they were Leighton Buzzard, Tring and Dunstable, but on the first morning, we were sent to Edlesborough, which was not far from Dunstable. It was all a bit confusing to start with, we had little idea why we were there, then a briefing revealed all. A man, Fairley, had broken into a house in the village, he was armed at the time. In this particular house he had raped the woman, as well as indecently assaulting her, then he had disappeared, his whereabouts was unknown. Senior Officers felt Fairley was still in the area, this was established when more offences were committed by him in the vicinity. It was decided that officers should be drafted in from other forces to help with the manhunt, Thames Valley was happy to provide PSU to work a night shift. Aerial surveillance and armed officers were used, but Fairley was undaunted by all this attention, he continued on his one-man crime wave.

Our PSU was brought into the search in April 1984, we went to Dunstable Police Station for a briefing before we started our shift, these briefings happened every night, which was not a bad idea, this allowed the officers on the enquiry to know what had happened during the day. The night shift was twelve hours long, we were normally paired up for our duty, a lot of the time this meant walking the streets of Edlesborough or possibly Dunstable. The people of those areas were advised not to come out at night, as well as securing their property. I do remember we were on foot patrol in the small village, we spoke to four other foot patrols, that made a total of ten officers patrolling the centre, and at that time the crime rate slumped to no crime at all, which was not surprising. My colleague and I were situated one night in the golf club, possibly the best duty, we had a clear view of the course itself, if anyone had moved we would have known about it.

There was a lot of chatter on the radio, people that were out and about were checked thoroughly. The firearms teams were completely out of sight, hiding in long grass or the likes. I do remember one of this team calling up and saying there was someone hiding in the grass not far from him, then a call came up from another team saying it was them. There were many false alarms, no doubt due to tiredness. I will now explain the sequence of events which this enquiry took, as I said this all happened in April 1984.

A 74-year-old woman, who lived alone, went to bed about 9 pm, this was near to Leighton Buzzard. For an hour she read peacefully, then she turned out the light. She was drifting off to sleep when she was aware of a shuffling noise, she opened her eyes and turned on the light and saw a man in her bedroom.

Holding a gloved hand in front of his face, the man pulled back the bed covers and indecently assaulted the woman. She bravely resisted his advances, so much so that he fled the scene. On the 10th May, he broke into a house in Cheddington, it was in fact the home of a 35-year-old single man, he was out visiting his girlfriend at the time of the break-in. Fairley stole £300 in cash, but more significantly he stole a shotgun and cartridges. Most burglars would have been happy to take the money and the gun, but not so with Fairley, he had been undetected and unchallenged, he decided to wait for the occupant to return. The owner returned at 11 pm to be faced with Fairley waiting for him, he was now wearing a mask and brandishing the gun. I will now call Fairley by his nickname, the Fox, hopefully, this will avoid any confusion. The Fox tied his victim up, then calmly played some pornographic videos, which we can only assume belonged to the victim, then the Fox indecently assaulted the man. When he left he buried the gun, but he buried it so well he was unable to find it at a later date.

After committing three more burglaries, the Fox broke into a house in Tring, again there was nobody at home, he carefully removed clothing from the drawers, along with photographs from an album, and once again found a shotgun with cartridges. This time he kept his find, which he would use when committing further crimes.

Just three days later he broke into a house at Heath and Reach, near Leighton Buzzard. Once again the occupants were out for the evening, this time the Fox decided to construct a lair and he would wait for his victims to return. He removed the light bulbs to ensure darkness, then he moved the furniture about, covering it with blankets, his aim was to watch videos without giving himself away. As he waited, he collected dressing gown cords and cut the telephone lines, and made an escape route for himself, then he helped himself to food from the fridge, and had a cup of tea.

At 1.30 am the occupants returned home, the Fox took fright and fled with £130 in cash, an anorak and a packet of peanuts, I am unaware of the significance of the peanuts, and what made him flee the scene having waited there all night. The occupants found the teapot was still warm. The Fox crossed the fields on foot to another house in Leighton Buzzard, the occupants, a married couple, were asleep when he appeared in their bedroom doorway brandishing the gun and wearing a mask, he appeared to terrify the occupants, which was not surprising. The male spotted him in the pale glow of the night light, he shouted at him. Whether by design or accident the gun went off and struck the man in the hand, this did not stop him chasing the Fox from the house, he left the anorak and the peanuts from the previous burglary. As the Fox later told the police, the gun going off scared him so much, he did not commit any further offences for a month, although he felt the injured man was more scared.

But then on the 6th July, unable to resist his newfound passion, he broke into a house in Linslade. Once again it was during the night, once again he was armed, once again there was a married couple in bed, asleep. They awoke to find the Fox pointing a gun at them. He ordered them out of the bed and tied them up with their own clothes and shoelaces. He indecently assaulted the wife, who screamed out, he panicked and fled the scene, unknown if he took any property. Just four days later he was at it again, breaking into a bungalow, occupied by a man and his wife, along with their two children, all were asleep in their beds. The couple awoke to find a man in their bedroom wearing a balaclava and pointing a shotgun at them. He told the wife to tie up her husband, which she reluctantly did, he then indecently assaulted her, this caused the husband to protest. The Fox then struck the husband with the gun, then he raped the wife, then he tied her up, then he left.

Now the Fox moved his activities to nearby Edlesborough, that was where our PSU first got involved, we had not been involved previously, mainly because it was another forces area, at that time they did not ask for our assistance. Our initial involvement meant going from house to house in the village, accompanied by an armed officer, trying to find out if the Fox was still located in any of the houses, it was a laborious task. He had committed burglaries in the village and broke into a bungalow on the 17th August, where he found an 18-year-old girl with her boyfriend and brother, the girl and her boyfriend were sleeping, while the brother was playing records. The brother saw the Fox, who was wearing a balaclava and carrying a shotgun. The girl awoke and was confronted by the Fox, all three were herded into the girl's bedroom, the boys were told to lie on the floor and were tied up with flex, the girl was tied up on the bed with a pillow over her head. The Fox went off for a drink, he then came back and raped the girl. He raped her again before stealing some videotapes, then he left.

The Fox then moved up to Milton Keynes, where he committed a series of burglaries. Then on 19th August, he decided to go to his native county of Durham, no doubt we were still looking for him in Hertfordshire. He drove up the M1, then onto the M18, the motorway that leads to the A1 and the North East of England. He still had the gun, he was obviously in the mood for more excitement, on the M18 he reversed his car onto the hard shoulder, he went into a wooded area on foot, he crossed the motorway and fields, before breaking into a house occupied by a man and a woman, this was in a small hamlet called Brampton-en-le-Morthen. Once again innocent people were awakened to find a masked man holding a gun. The couple were tied together by one l assaulted the leg, he searched the house and then indecently assaulted the woman. He raped the woman before calmly cutting out a square of bedding, ensuring semen-stained material would not fall into the hands of the police. On returning to his car the Fox decided to hide the mask and the gun, as well as a pair of gloves, an act which would result in his no small way to his ultimate downfall. He had a slight accident in his car when he reversed into some bushes, paintwork was left at the scene, fragments of paint was on the branches. He then drove to Peterlee near Sunderland, where he committed two more similar crimes. He later returned to Leighton Buzzard area, where he committed a further eleven offences at Milton Keynes.

We went to Dunstable each night to be briefed, we were not quite sure where the Fox was, but we continued our observations, hoping to catch this man sooner rather than later, the longer the search went on, the more damage he was causing.

Forensic material became very helpful, the paint fragments left in the woods belonged to a British Leyland harvest yellow car, all models were checked, the name of Malcolm Fairley appeared on the list of owners. At his house in Kentish Town, London, detectives saw he was cleaning his car, they saw the scratched paintwork. They found overalls with a leg missing, that leg piece of material was used to make a mask.

Fairley was promptly arrested by detectives; he reportedly broke down and confessed to all the crimes on the journey to the police station. Fairley was arrested on the

11th September at his home address in London. He was tried at St. Albans Crown Court on the 26th February 1985, he was sentenced to six life sentences for the attacks, plus a further 26 years in prison for related offences, this totalled 146 years imprisonment.

It appears that Fairley has been released from prison under a new identity, less than 20 years into his sentence, I have no idea how that came about, it seems a useless exercise to give scumbags long sentences. Fairley was sentenced in February 1985, the following is what Justice Caulfield said at the time,

"There are degrees of wickedness beyond condemnatory description. Your crimes fall within this category. You desecrated and defiled men and women in their own homes. You are a decadent advertisement for evil pornographers."

One of the saddest days was Wednesday 19th August 1987, I was on early turn at the time, as it got close to 2 pm, my end of shift, we were told to wait upstairs. My whole shift was in the bar upstairs watching the news on the television, it spoke of someone going berserk in Hungerford, we watched the television hoping to get more details, and we had nothing else to do. Hungerford was a small town in Berkshire, no doubt the name will ring bells, I remember it as a terrible day in this country's history, it was also a day when firearms law was changed. I had only been in the Police for eight years in 1987, an incident like this was new to me. It was thought we might be required in Hungerford, that was the reason we waited around. The name of the person who had committed these atrocities in Hungerford was one Michael Ryan. We remained in the bar watching the news, I cannot remember where the information came from, it could have been from the news, or maybe it was from our headquarters. It was I believe just before 6 pm when we were told that Ryan had committed suicide, he was in a classroom on the first floor, in the school he attended in his youth, there he shot himself. I do not feel the people of Hungerford were in any way saddened to hear of his death. We were stood down from the bar, I was going to Hungerford the following day with our PSU, it might seem strange to go there after he had committed suicide, but the idea was to keep the general public and the press away from the carnage, only people who lived in the village were allowed in.

Ryan had left his house in 4 South View having caught the house on fire, I believe he had shot his mother and she was inside the house, although I cannot be sure of that fact. He shot his two next-door neighbours, fatally wounding them in the process. When people started to hear about what had happened in Hungerford, they were unaware that Ryan had already murdered Susan Godfrey in Savernake Wood earlier in the day, she had been shot many times in the back, it is believed this was witnessed by her children. Ryan then made his way to Hungerford; his day of killing had only just begun.

It was fortunate that Thames Valley firearms team were training at Kidlington, the Force headquarters, I believe they were taken to Hungerford by police helicopter, although I cannot confirm that, it was something that was said. The Firearm team arrived sometime after all the killing had finished, except one, that was when Ryan shot himself, there was very little sadness about that. In total Ryan killed 16 innocent people, there were many more who survived, remaining in their houses as Ryan shot at the houses, the bullet holes could be seen clearly when we went there the following day. One of those killed was PC Roger Brereton, I believe he was the area beat officer for Hungerford, he went to Ryan's house to assess the fire, he made a short message to the control room. What he said was that someone was at the back of the car, he had a gun in his hand, that was the last message from Roger, the sound of the shot being fired was also recorded.

It is not certain exactly when Ryan made his way to the school, bearing in mind the streets were empty, although he was being watched by a few brave members of the public, his whereabouts was being passed to the police. The problem was that he was moving around the town, once someone told the police where he was, he was gone, it was not easy to keep track of him. I cannot be sure when Ryan made his way to the school, which fortunaely the pupils were on summer holidays, so he was there on his own, he was in a classroom on the first floor. By this time the Firearms team had arrived, they positioned themselves with a view of the classroom, but they were limited as to what they could do. They could only fire if the officer with a gun was in danger or a member of the public were in danger, neither scenario fitted the bill, it was a case of waiting for Ryan to make a move, which he did not do. A gunshot was heard from the school, it was assumed Ryan had shot himself, but the police had to be certain, so they sent a dog into the room. It was assumed if Ryan was alive he would have shot the dog, there were no more shots and the dog returned safely to his handler. The police approached the classroom, tied a rope or the likes around Ryan's ankles and pulled him out. The press, acting in their usual selfish manner, wanted to know why the marksmen had not shot Ryan when he came into view in the classroom, the reason for shooting was explained to them, had the officer shot him it would have been murder. I know it is a strange set of laws when you consider what Ryan had done, but that the law. I feel sure Ryan wanted the police to shoot him, he lingered near the window of the classroom, when he realised this was not going to happen, he finished the job himself. The police were also criticised by the press for dragging out the body, they felt it was undignified until the police explained, he might have had a grenade or something similar, this would explode as soon as the body was moved. What it did show about the press, they thought they knew better than the police, obviously, none of them had given service to their country. While we were there the Prime Minister was on her way down, this being Margaret Thatcher, she came into the town, she thanked everyone for what they had done, offering her condolences to the people of the town. It was a strange village, but everyone in the village knew someone who had been killed, there was nothing we could say to make their grief easier to deal with, but we were there trying to help. We left at the end of the day, never to return.

Our PSU also spent a lot of Saturday afternoons at Oxford United's football ground, that was the season they had been promoted to the Premier League, quite an achievement, but it caused a few problems, this was mainly because the ground was too small. Many of the Premier League clubs had away support that would fill Oxford's ground, and I do not think the visiting fans were aware of that. At every game there were away fans locked out, they were not happy about it, which was understandable, many had travelled hundreds of miles to get to the game, I appreciate they should have bought a ticket first. Of all the games Oxford played at home to Premier League sides, there was one that stood, not for their football skills, but their fans caused the most trouble. You may be surprised to hear it was Coventry City, maybe some of those so-called fans are proud of that, I know there were fans all over the country causing problems, they were not the brightest.

We did occasionally Police Reading's home games, one I remember vividly was against Arsenal, it was an FA Cup match, the ground was packed full to bursting point, but there was no trouble, the fans were a credit to the town.

I went to one game as a civilian, it was a local derby at Reading, it was against Oxford United. There was a group of yobs standing around, they did not seem to have an interest in the game, then I realised why, they were looking for people to assault. I had obviously been picked out, they sent a girl over to speak to me, she said I sounded like I came from Oxford. I escorted her back to her friends, showing them my warrant card, and emphasising the young lady was an idiot if she thought my accent was from Oxford, but to be honest they all were all idiots. I am not sure my chat served any purpose, perhaps she was the brains of the operation. The group consisted of eight young men and the girl, they had targetted me, someone on their own, how brave are these football fans. I think most of the football yobs were like that, the odds had to be in their favour, cowards is the correct name for them. I spoke to the sergeant covering the game, pointing out this group in full view of them, that might have put them off, they were now being watched, or so they thought. During my career I have often come across the yob element, they were people who went looking for a fight, providing the odds were in their favour, they never favoured the one on one scenario.

We did have events to go to which were enjoyable, being part of the crowd without expecting trouble. This place was the Milton Keynes Bowl, it is still there but I do not know if it is used anymore. On the first occasion I went the main attraction was the group Thin Lizzy, which I enjoyed, but there was not too much room for the fans, it was on grass terraces, not quite the same as the crowds at Wembley arena. The group thanked us at the end of the concert, they were famous in their day. This venue must have been used before Wembley, I cannot remember the big groups today performing anywhere other than Wembley. There was one person who performed at the Bowl, he was a step above the rest, the late great Michael Jackson, a real superstar. My colleague had the prize job, he had to look after Michael during the concert, he told me later that he enjoyed it very much, whether he was given any souvenirs, I did not ask. It was not surprising that the Bowl was packed that night, he was a success, nobody expected anything else.

Early morning, Summer, 1984 in a field near Tring.
Officers after the Fox.

The arrest of Malcom Farley, aka 'The Fox', in London.
September 13th, 1984.

FOUR

The Miners' Dispute

In 1984 the country was thrown into turmoil by the coal miners strike. Many stories about the strike have been written, I will now tell it from the point of view of the officers who were there, no lies or stories, just the facts as to what happened. Why did it happen and why did the government of the day fail to sort out the problem before it got out of hand, that is relatively easy to explain. A certain leader of the miners wanted a strike, he had brought down the Heath government some years earlier, he thought it would be simple to bring down Margaret Thatcher's government, he could not have been more wrong. Perhaps the following facts relating to the government's handling of the crisis might assist the reader to reach a satisfactory conclusion. I will also explain the police organisation during the dispute, and the behaviour of those on the picket line.

The Reason for the Strike

In March 1984 it was announced that the Cortonwood pit, near Barnsley, was to close. On the 5th March, the miners at Cortonwood and all those Yorkshire pits walked out, followed by the news the next day that Cortonwood was one of 20 pits to close, putting 20,000 miners out of work. The man tasked with the government job was Peter Walker, the Energy Secretary. The Prime Minister, Margaret

Thatcher, was fully aware that the NUM leader was looking for confrontation. On three occasions during the previous government, Scargill had tried, unsuccessfully, to bring the miners out on strike. He was definitely thinking back to the 1970s, hoping he could again get the leader to resign. The government's point of view was that some pits were not productive enough, those pits had to close so the remaining pits could be modernised, thereby making those pits more efficient, not an unreasonable idea. There was the added bonus that no miners would be made redundant, and early retirement could be an option for some of the miners. A mobility allowance was offered to those who had to move pits, as well as a generous pay increase. There would be an investment of £800 million to modernise the remaining pits. It did seem a reasonable offer, so the terms were put to the cabinet, who agreed it was a good deal, and if the miners voted for it, then the deal would be accepted.

Unfortunately, the government was wrong, not that the offer was rejected in a ballot, for the first time the NUM did not hold a ballot, the miners were never asked to vote. It was Scargill who brought the miners out on strike, without any sort of ballot, the first time in NUM history, it was an unprecedented move. It appears Scargill was frightened to put it to a ballot, the deal the government offered would probably have been accepted by the miners. Nine coalfields did vote, against the wishes of the NUM, eight of them decided not to strike in their vote. At the time of the strike, no union in the country backed the strike, this included the Labour party, believing the strike to be unlawful without a ballot. It appeared to the onlooker this was not a strike about Pay and Conditions, nor was it for industrial reasons, it was for political reasons, instigated by Arthur Scargill. The demands made by Scargill are unbelievable, he did not want any pit closures, even if the pit was losing money, he just wanted all the miners to be working, although it was unlikely that his reasons had anything to do with the miners. Scargill was trying to bring down the government again, this time the government was stronger, he underrated the lady in charge, a decision he would come to regret.

Margaret Thatcher had already taken on the Print Industry and the Steel workers, she had a hit list of collieries she felt should close, most of which were in South Wales, but she withdrew from any action, no doubt on the advice of her Ministers. Unfortunately, the question arose again in respect of the coal mines, the subsidies they were paid caused a considerable strain on the Exchequers funds, something had to be done, sooner rather than later. The Government saw the NUM as the stronghold of a kind of Trade Union that was the curse of the country, the fact that Margaret Thatcher and Arthur Scargill did not like each other, did not help the situation at all. It is believed that if these two had not locked horns, and the strike had never taken place, the £10-£30 million which the strike was alleged to have cost, could have been used in the modernisation of the pits, maybe even keeping some of the closed pits open.

The economics at the time did not look good, following the demise of the Steel industry, the demand for coal fell sharply, this particularly affected the South Wales coalfields, hence the thought of closing them prior to the miners' strike. Perhaps something should have been put in place before any announcements were made, possibly a gradual closure of the uneconomical pits first, and strenuous attempts to find work for those laid off, but would that have been successful, I fear not. Arthur Scargill stuck to his guns, wanting all the pits to remain open, he did not really want to discuss the matter, there seemed little choice, the Government had to face up to the call for an all-out strike by the miners. Arthur Scargill got what he wanted, a platform on which he could preach his gospel, allowing Margaret Thatcher to flex her muscles.

The Law and Trade Disputes

If a threat of industrial action is unavoidable, it is up to the Local Authority to decide what response should be taken. Essentially the Local Authority should have a clear understanding of the law and the effects of Industrial Action, there are certain questions they must ask. Firstly, does it meet with the requirements of a trade dispute, which might thereby make the dispute immune from any sort of prosecution. Did the miner's dispute fit into the category of immunity? It is for you to decide when you have read the text. Industrial action is likely to be unlawful at Common Law, as the organisers are likely to commit at least one offence. In the case of the miners, it should be noted that individuals were induced to break their contracts with the pit owners, if in fact there was such a contract. Under these circumstances the Trade Union would be wide open to a claim of damages from the individuals and the employers, both who would lose money as a result of Industrial Action, was that the case with the miners and Pit owners?

However, in recognising the legal role of Industrial Action, Parliament introduced a degree of protection for Trade Unions, subject to many complicated and contentious criteria. The protection takes the form of Statutory Immunities from proceedings under which Industrial Action is classed as lawful. It is explained below whether an action is lawful or not, I hope this meets with your approval.

Whether a Strike is Official or Unofficial

In order that Industrial Action can be classed as Official, it must be approved by the Trade Union. This means that approval can be given by any official employed by the Union, in this case, Arthur Scargill, if he was elected by Union Rules, which he was. There is a mechanism in place that states the President or General Secretary can cancel that action, but this does not apply to Arthur Scargill, who was at the time the General Secretary of the Union. So, any mechanism in place to stop this Industrial Action was ineffective, as Arthur Scargill had a position of power in the Union. Therefore, the action he took should be classed as being legal. Section 219 of TULR c A provides certain immunities, but they can be removed under the following circumstances.

a) Action amounts to unlawful picketing, balloting requirement has not yet been met, we will discuss this later.

b) Action can amount to unlawful secondary action.

c) Statutory balloting requirement has not yet been met, something already mentioned on the previous page.

These are not all the requirements, but only the one's likely to affect the Miner's Dispute. So that Industrial Action can be lawful it must be taken in the following circumstances.

A Trade Dispute is defined as a dispute between workers and their employers, which relates wholly or mainly to one or more of a number of specified matters.

As in B above we turn to Secondary Action, except for lawful picketing, it can be classed as unlawful, if the following criteria is met. Lawful picketing is a form of Secondary action which is lawful. Provided the strict provisions are adhered to in full. Pickets must picket at or near to their own workplace, surely as in the Miner's Dispute, to picket a pit in Yorkshire, when you work in a pit in Nottinghamshire, does not fit the criteria. It did happen, along with an influx of Welsh miners, maybe they got lost going to work, so unlawful picketing happened all over Yorkshire and Nottinghamshire. Picketing must also be limited to peaceful persuasion to any person to work or not to work, throwing bricks at the police vehicles taking miners to work, does not fit that criteria. A Trade Dispute must be wholly or mainly related to specific points, as in the Miner's Dispute, Scargill did not want any pits to close, he knew these closures had to take place, but he wanted to pursue the lost cause as long as possible. It was his way of ensuring the strike continued, demanding something that would not happen, he must have known that, but he made sure the miners would strike for a year. Hopefully, the previous pages have explained a little of the background to the law in respect of Trade Disputes. Whether Scargill met the criteria laid down, I will leave you to decide that, I think he used the strike to further his own career, but you may disagree with me.

Arthur Scargill

Arthur Scargill was born on the 11th January 1938 in Worsbrough Dale, West Riding of Yorkshire. He was President of the NUM from 1982 until 2002. He joined the NUM at the age of 19 in 1957, he became one of its leading activists in the late 1960s. He led the unofficial strike in 1969 and played a key role in organising the strikes of 1972 and 1974, the latter helped in the downfall of Edward Heath's Conservative Government. His views are described as Marxist.

A decade later, he led the NUM through the 1984-1985 miners strike, a major event in the history of the British Labour movement. It turned into a confrontation with the Conservative Government, led by Margaret Thatcher, with which the NUM were defeated, although many miners still think they won. More will be mentioned later about Mr Scargill's life.

Policing the Pits

This is my story of the year-long dispute, starting in March 1984, when our PSU, Police Support Unit, was transported to Ollerton Colliery in Nottingham. This colliery was the scene of the unfortunate death of a picket a few days earlier, his name was David Jones. We were briefed about the incident, although we were all aware of the tragedy, and advised that our actions would be monitored as a result of the incident, none of us wanted to show any disrespect to the fallen miner.

We left Buckinghamshire at 4 am, travelling to Nottingham by hired coach, cold and not fully aware of what awaited us, we arrived at Ollerton at mid-morning. We did not have any police transits available, we were somewhat confused with the situation, not really knowing why we were there, but then few of us had been on a picket line before, it was all very new. There were just a few pickets at the gate when we arrived, they did not appear to be causing any problems. We stayed on the thin picket line all day, travelling back home in the late afternoon, slightly confused by the whole thing, the miners who were there did not show any animosity towards us. We discussed the situation in the coach travelling home, what we had seen at Ollerton, made us think the dispute would be over in a couple of weeks, how wrong that was to prove, but our judgement was only based on what we had seen at the pit that day. On that first day, we were dressed in normal uniform, tunics and lightweight helmets, oblivious to how events would drastically change our appearance, our views on the dispute were yet to come.

Our first port of call during the strike, after the day at Ollerton, was Bilsthorpe Colliery in Nottingham, this was at the beginning of the strike, and we were staying for a week. I had the feeling the strike had not taken hold in South Yorkshire, but I may be wrong about that. I am not sure if there were pickets on the gate, but we were welcomed by miners, I later found out they were the safety men who were not allowed to go on strike, the pit was at least partly operational. It was quiet outside so the safety man asked if anyone wanted to have a look at the coalface, we all volunteered for that.

Before making the descent we donned overalls, hard hats with working lamps. I remember quite vividly the journey downwards in a wire cage, I could feel the air coming up. It took some time in the cage, then we moved onto the next part of the journey, this was on a small train, then we went onto the conveyor belt, forever moving downwards, our guide went to great lengths to explain the conveyor belt. We changed belts several times, our guide led and told us to get off when he did, we followed his example, we did not lose anyone. The belt took us into the lower depths of the mine, continually travelling downwards on a flimsy belt, waiting to be told to get off, the words eventually came. The journey took several hours, the temperature rising the lower we got, until we reached the coal face, to everyone's joy and relief. I remember watching the large circular cutting ripping into the coal face, the area was propped up by wooden beams, substantial enough to do the job I hoped, no doubt the miners thought the same. There were miners working in this part of the pit, they were bent over as they raked out the coal deposits. The trip taught me one crucial thing, I did not fancy the coal miners job, the conditions were unbelievable, but it was the way they got to work, along with the amount of time it took them to get there. My story moves ahead to June, but I suspect we had visited other pits which I cannot remember at this stage.

It was June 18th 1984, we were sent to Orgreave Coking Plant near Scunthorpe, this was the day that changed everything for the police, in the minds of the police officers who stood in that field at Orgreave. Transported there in the early hours of the morning, at that stage we had no protective gear, it was our normal uniform, I do not think anyone expected trouble, we arrived to be confronted by thousands of pickets. I believe the local officers had on riot gear, they just forgot to tell the rest of the police. The newsreels said that rioters had clashed with police in riot gear, I am not sure where this took place, the majority of officers had no riot gear. Why should the newsreels lie about that, the answer is simple, it made a better story, but we knew the truth. If the clips of Orgreave are examined, there are several in this book, showing police officers were not in riot gear, but then lying is an occupation the press are good at, I will explain another incident later. The media also reported that 84 pickets had been arrested, I am surprised there were not more. Perhaps the media failed to notice that the pickets were throwing bricks and stones, pieces of wood, and virtually anything else they could get their hands, they were not concerned about injuring unprotected officers, and neither were the press. Eventually, the horses were brought in to push the miners back, making sure they were out of range from throwing missiles at officers. The miners used the horses as an excuse, this was the police attacking the miners, nothing was mentioned of the stone-throwing, which caused injuries to a lot of officers, how come the media failed to notice that. It was obvious the media were on the side of the miners, it was obvious to all of us. Arthur Scargill was arrested that day, he said he had been hit by a police shield, that was very unlikely, like a general he was too far back and was protected on all sides, but saying that made the headlines. He hoped by making the allegation the charge might be dropped, it had many years ago, it is an old trick, but it did not work this time. As I said Orgreave changed everything, it was obvious the miners had no intention of carrying out peaceful picketing, so the police changed tactics, all those on duty at the pits were issued with riot gear and shields. We did not intend to suffer the casualties we had suffered at Orgreave, although nobody ever knew about the casualties, the press did not print things like that. Now we were ready, the softly approach had not worked. Whether there was some sort of an agreement among the miners to use a certain level of violence against the police is unclear, but I felt sure it was organised at some level.

On the Miners' Dispute in riot gear without the sheilds.

Orgreave Coking Plant.
Officers in normal uniform, not riot gear, but that didn't stop the miners from throwing stones and bricks at the unprotected officers.

Orgreve Coking Plant.
The behaviour of miners brought about the need for officers to wear riot gear from then onwards.

Cortonwood Colliery

This was where it all began, or so the rumours say. It was originally announced that Cortonwood would be one of the pits that was going to closed. This brought about a decision to strike, although no ballot was taken, but as already stated the rules state that a ballot was not needed. I cannot recall if Cortonwood was one of the first pits to close, I suspect it probably was.

Beecholme Holiday Camp, Cleethorpes

During the months we looked after the pits in South Yorkshire, we were accommodated at the above site in Cleethorpes. We were not allowed to stay in Yorkshire, so they housed us several hours away. The strange irony of the situation was that miners stayed at the holiday camp before the strike, but that did not continue after we left, the owner sold up knowing the circumstances of the police staying there. I am sure in that year he made a lot of money from the police services throughout the country.

The camp itself was made up of chalets, cheaply built to cater for summer trade, they were very cold inside, which meant we put the cooker on to keep ourselves warm. These chalets were two bedroomed, with enough beds for five people, which was the exact number of officers in a shield unit. Three officers at the front carrying shields, two behind with medical equipment and a fire extinguisher. Each shield unit stayed together in one chalet. The chalets had wafer-thin walls, which was not ideal in the winter months, but we spent very little time there, the east coast in winter was a chilly place. This was the first time we had left the force area for more than a day, this brought certain regulations into play. We found out that working away from your force area, we were entitled to sixteen hours pay a day, this meant eight hours overtime each day, hence the rumours about how much the police had been paid. Once the strike got into its stride, each PSU went up to South Yorkshire every fortnight, leaving at lunchtime on the Sunday and returning late Friday evening. On our arrival at the holiday camp, we were shown our billets, then we went to the briefing, that was about 7 pm. The briefing was to let you know which pit you would be policing for that week; it was relevant to where you billet was located. The whole thing was organised with precision, I believe it was done at New Scotland Yard. The dining room on camp was open at 10.30 pm for breakfast, yes, the time was correct. Once we had eaten we prepared to go onto the road and head towards South Yorkshire, we had to leave by midnight, the trip could take up to four hours, depending on where your pit was along the route. The transits travelled in a specific order, the ones who had the furthest to travel were at the front, going back in order to the one who left the convoy first. On the route we had motorcycle outriders, I believe they were from Leicestershire Police, they did a terrific job, if we got to a town they stopped traffic so we could get through without stopping. The convoy usually consisted of forty to fifty transit vans, full of police officers, heading across the middle of the country, I should imagine it was quite a sight. As each pit was reached, transits dropped off the rear of the convoy, the convoy kept decreasing as we went along, it was a well-organised operation. I know that each pit finished at different times; I think this allowed us to make our own way back to the holiday camp. I believe the reason we did not stay in South Yorkshire was political, the local officers had to police the area when we left, it would have made life more difficult for them, we all understood that. When those at the top appreciated we were being paid for all those hours, they did their best to ensure we worked sixteen hours a day. It was obvious we would spend little time in the accommodation, most of our sleep was gained in the back of the transit, either going to the pit or coming back. It became common practice to take your pillow in the transit, sometimes a blanket was needed. The driver, who could not sleep, was not required on the picket line, he slept in the transit while we were away. Several of the pits stick in my mind, the events that happened there, and the comradeship of the officers you were with, not all police officers would have been good on a PSU, but the ones that went were good officers. It was strange, and sometimes difficult, to deal with the violent situation we came across on the picket line, but deal with it we did, because we had the right men doing the job.

We visited Cortonwood again, not a particularly riveting experience, we were there for a week, there was a melee of pickets, some pushing and shoving, the usual abuse, nothing to really report. It was where the strike started, but there was nothing happening on the week we spent there.

Yorkshire Main

We made several visits to this pit, the pickets were very verbal, there was always the likelihood of violence, but it never materialised. There were no serious disturbances worth noting.

Silverwood Colliery

I believe we only visited this colliery once, yet another uneventful week, plenty of pickets and plenty of noise, but no major disturbances, except on one occasion. Several of the pickets took exception to what someone said, they were agitated by one particular picket, a few punches were thrown, then it was all over. Silverwood did eventually close, I believe it was 1987.

Rossington Colliery

Yet another one week stand, there were packed audiences, the usual shouting, but nothing other than that to report. The threats towards us at all the pits were there, but very little came of it. The usual main threats appeared on the Friday, I will explain that later. I do not have the details of when Rossington closed.

Kiveton Park Colliery

This was a favourite with our PSU, we had been based at this pit on many occasions, it was also the preferred pit for trouble, something our PSU had a reputation for dealing with, or at least that was what the Senior Officers in South Yorkshire believed.

It one on one of these occasions, following the usual pushing and shoving by the pickets, there was a lull in the action, we stood around in a group chatting, I had my back to the pickets who were about 40 metres away, this action seemed to upset the pickets, they did not like being ignored. As if from a Laurel and Hardy film, my colleague who was standing directly in front of me, received an egg straight in the middle of his forehead, it broke and ran down over his nose, the pickets cheered. The accuracy of the shot was unnerving, we all found it difficult to keep a straight face, although the officer was livid and wanted revenge, wishful thinking on his part. There were always large groups of pickets at Kiveton Park, it was used on several Fridays for the end of the week mass picketing, the name of the pit to be picketed did not get revealed until Thursday. The miners used their telephones to pass the information to other miners, believing their telephones had been tapped, there was no need for that, there were undercover police officers picketing with the miners, they knew the location of the mass picket on Thursday, that was passed to our headquarters. The pickets tried to feed false information of the mass picketing over the phone, still believing it was tapped, it was strange that we always turned up at the right pit that was carrying out the mass picketing, the miners never quite worked that one out. The reason for Friday was simple, it was the day all officers returned to their home force, the idea was to delay this return, so each week the decided pit carried out mass picketing. There were two things wrong with this, officers would earn more money if delayed, something the miners complained about, the second was we knew which pit was going to be picketed. The pickets will tell you that security was important, their security was very flawed, we knew the pit for mass picketing on the same day as the miners.

On one occasion at Kiveton Park the pickets were pushing against the shields, the frustration got the better of one of the pickets, he decided to hit the inspector, a tragic mistake on his part. He was taken out of the line of miners, passed between the shields and duly arrested for the assault, he was surprised how quickly this was done, he had time to think over his stupid decision.

A few months later he appeared at Mansfield Magistrates, he pleaded not guilty to the charge. When the case came to Court, he had four witnesses, our inspector only had two, the case was adjourned as the inspector stated he could have brought more witnesses. When we turned up a few weeks later he was on his own, he had returned to work, but his witnesses had not, they refused to testify for him. He changed his plea to guilty and was dealt with, it was a fine I believe, it was a large one, he was not happy, whether that was because his associates had failed to turn up, I did not know.

As I have already said Kiveton Park was used on many occasions for mass picketing, some of those arrested came from South Wales, some from Kent, I believe we also had a Scotsman, but we believed he had just got lost. These pickets showed a complete disregard for the flying picket syndrome, I think they thought they were allowed to do it. The idea was that you could picket your own pit only, hence the term Flying Picket announced its arrival into our vocabulary. Kiveton Park closed in 1994.

Maltby Colliery

Maltby Collier came under the jurisdiction of Rotherham. This colliery reared its head in the later days of the dispute, it was not somewhere our PSU had visited before, I cannot remember when we were on duty there. We received information that Maltby was going to be the pit on Friday, when mass picketing was to take place. It proved a memorable location in many ways, as the following story will relay to you. Firstly, I must explain the layout of the picketing. The pickets were along a road, it had woods on either side, we arrived and parked the transit in the car park and then march down to the picket line. The senior officer told our inspector to take us to the front, which he did. At this point we only heard a lot of noise, we could not see the pickets, I believe it was about 3 am, it was pitch black. Some large lights were sent for, giving us some idea of how many pickets we were dealing with. The lights arrived and were shone down the road, all we could see was pickets, they made it clear they did not like the lights being shone on them. There were then stones being thrown at us, they were not big but they could cause damage to the facial area, we realised where the stones had come from, it was the wooded area on either side of the road. The light, called a dragon light, was shone down the road, it is difficult to estimate how many pickets there were, but there were several thousand. They were about 50 feet from our front line, which was in fact our PSU. Once again the stones started to come, but the problem was quickly solved, several police dogs were sent into the wooded area, there was a lot of growling, followed by a lot of screaming. The pickets left the wooded area, never to return, mainly because they had been arrested by the dog handlers.

It was then that a decision was made for us to draw our truncheons, these were special truncheons, about three foot long, and moved forward about 20 feet, hopefully, the miners would move back, which they did. I looked around me and saw about 100 officers on the picket line, if the pickets decided to chance their arm and attack us, we would have suffered major injuries. Once the pickets moved back we tried to move forward again, the pickets retreated. At no point did we reach the pickets, but that was not important to the newsreels. That night we watched the local news, it showed the point when we drew our truncheons and moved forward, once again the many hours we were being stoned did not appear, obviously not newsworthy. Since that day I have believed little of any outside broadcast shown on the television, they are not in any way neutral, they take the side that proves an interesting news item, not to be trusted I am afraid. After several hours of stalemate, the pickets started to disperse, once they had gone we marched back to the car park, that was when we all got a surprise, there were about fifty transits full of police officers, that was about 500 officers standing by. The news said there were 15,000 pickets there, I could not see them all, but I was sure there was a lot, why should the newsreel lie? So the truth, and the news, are two different organisms, what a shame the news is believed by many people, but they have never been in a position to see when they are lying.

Elsecar Workshops

This was, without doubt, my favourite picket line, this was mainly due to the fact there were no pickets, it turned out to be an easy week, something we did not know about. We still did our sixteen hours a day, but there was a great deal of sleeping, it was good to be paid to sleep, that was the best part of it. I am not sure how we got fed, I am not sure there was anyone at the workshops, had we been sent to the wrong place, I cannot remember the feeding arrangements but I am sure we were fed.

We went upstairs and found an office, it was carpeted throughout, many of us decided to sleep on the floor, bringing out blankets and pillows from the transit.

Whilst at Elsecar a colleague phoned his girlfriend, she was working in Paris, he found a telephone and took advantage of the situation, he spoke to her for about thirty minutes. I have no doubt that when the phone bill eventually arrives, enquiries would be carried out to find the culprit. Nothing was ever mentioned about the bill, I expect the National Coal Board paid.

Many historians have provided interpretations and explanations for the Miner's defeat in the 1984-1985 dispute. You may be interested to read some of these comments.

Robert Taylor depicts Arthur Scargill as an Industrial Napoleon, who called a strike at the wrong time, it was also on the wrong issue, and adapted strategies and tactics that were impossible to fulfil. He had an inflexible list of extravagant non-negotiable demands, it amounted to a dangerous self-defeating delusion.

Numerous scholars have concluded that Scargill's decisive tactical error was to substitute his famous flying picket for the holding of a national strike ballot. His policy alienated most of the Nottinghamshire miners, undermining his position with the leaders of the trade union movement, hurting the union's reputation in British public opinion, and led to violence along the picket line. That violence strengthened the stature of the Coal Board and the Thatcher government.

There were two other pits we went to which I remember quite well, the first was Grimethorpe Colliery, that was where a famous brass band performed, but they did not perform on the days we visited. It was a pit where very little happened, there were pickets of course, usually quite noisy, but they did not cause us any major problems. The next pit was a bit problematic.

We arrived at Goldthorpe Colliery one day when we were on a roaming brief, that basically meant we were not designated to a particular pit, we went to any pit where there was trouble, and there was trouble at Goldthorpe. On arrival on the picket line, we were faced with a few pickets causing trouble, they started to throw stones at us, along with anything they could get hold of, they were out to cause trouble. It did not concern us too much, we had our shields. But for one miner it was a mistake to throw stones at us, he was easily recognisable, he had a plaster on his left leg, he was wearing a tracksuit over the plaster, which was split up the side. Everyone in our PSU made a note of this character, we hoped we would see him again. The crowd started to disperse, we looked for the man with the plaster, he was nowhere to be seen, a sensible move to disappear. The trouble was he did not disappear, our sergeant saw him on the wall further up the street, myself and a colleague went up to find him, there he was sitting on a wall talking. We pulled him off the wall and arrested him, this caused boos from the crowd. He was taken back to a local police station where he was charged. He obviously never had the sense he was born with, taking part in a riot with a plaster on your leg, he was taken to Barnsley, he continued to declare his innocence on the way to the station. It took some time before the case came to court, our man had decided to plead not guilty, he took top marks for stupidity, he had made a strange decision. The defence solicitor asked me how far up his leg did the plaster go, I said I did not know, he then told me it went up to his knee, did that surprise me. Questions like this showed his solicitor was struggling somewhat, but that was nothing to the one question he asked my colleague, he wanted to know where the transit was parked, my colleague looked a little confused with the question. He could not remember exactly, the solicitor sat down with a smile on his face, I think he may have been dealing with another case, I cannot think of any reason why the solicitor would think he had defended this man correctly. He was found guilty and fined, his solicitor should have paid the fine. The two pits were closed within a year of each other, Grimethorpe in 1993, and Goldthorpe a year later, in 1994.

After the miner's strike Arthur Scargill was elected lifetime president of the NUM, he won by an overwhelming national majority, in a controversial election. He stood down from his leadership role in July 2002, he became the honorary president. He was succeeded by Ian Lavery.

In 1990, Scargill was accused of mishandling money donated to the miner's strike. It was also alleged that, the money donated by Libya, some was used to give himself a bridging loan, as well as money towards his home, he gave £10,000 to the striking Nottinghamshire miners. He also received money from Russia for the Welsh miners, this was placed in a Dublin bank for the "International Miners Organisation", where it stayed until a year after the strike had finished. He obviously had some suspicious friends,

Libya and Russia, that are the only ones we know about. There was much criticism of Scargill within the NUM, from the Welsh and Scottish miners.

In July 1990 the NUM executive voted unanimously to sue Scargill and the General Secretary at the time. Negotiations between Scargill and the NUM took place in secret in France. In September 1990, criminal charges were brought against Scargill for wilfully neglecting to perform the union's duty to keep proper accounting records. Scargill reached an agreement to repay the money to the NUM.

To return to my story, we were on one occasion billeted at Sheffield University, it must have been in the summer, as the students were not there, it was luxury for us, single bedrooms. There was a five-a-side court, we took advantage of that, but not everyone had the correct footwear, there was a mass changing of shoes at the end of each game.

Once the miner's dispute was in full swing, the feeding of officers improved greatly, this included being provided with a bag, it contained sandwiches, a chocolate bar, and possibly a piece of fruit, but I cannot be sure of the fruit, but this was on top of our regular meals. We decided on one of the weeks to have an eating competition. The inspector made up a group of rules before we started, they were as follows:

All meals put in front of the officer had to be consumed. If a meal was offered from another source, that had to be eaten. For some strange reason that week we were offered more food than normal. On one occasion someone in our PSU arrested a miner, he was to be taken to Mansfield Police Station, where we were told there was a meal if anyone wanted it. All those still in the competition had to go to Mansfield, there were six of us still left in. I cannot imagine what the prisoner thought, he was being escorted by six officers, he must have thought he was a master criminal, we never mentioned the eating competition. This competition went on all week, there were two officers left at the end, it was sorted out on the bus going home, it required the competitors to eat sandwiches, about six each I believe. Who won the competition I have no idea, but I do know that I put on weight that week.

The dispute was coming to an end in Yorkshire, we were given a night off, that meant a visit to the local dance halls of Cleethorpes, or as we called it, grab a granny night. To be fair it was the bar that was the big attraction, there were about fifty officers who attended the dance, we all behaved of course, the bar did a roaring trade. As far as the grannies were concerned, there were only two of them in the dance hall, they looked pleased by the abundance of men, but I believe their luck was out. We left South Yorkshire the following day, we would not be returning.

Two weeks later we were sent to Durham, they had mines under the sea, most of the miners were back at work, those who were picketing were very friendly, and we were working a day shI still have no idea why we were sent to Durham, but I did not care, I was being well paid for doing next to nothing. When we left Durham the dispute was over, it had been a very long year.

At the beginning of the dispute, when we were in Nottingham, we were left in a large hall with a television and tea making facilities. I do not think the organisers knew what to do with us. On the first a motorcyclist came in and asked if anyone was watching the television, there was someone I said they were not, not sure what channel he was going to put on, but he did not change channels. Instead of that, he put a video into the machine, suddenly everyone's attention was drawn to the television. Our motorcyclist had put on a pornographic film, the hall fell quiet. Each morning our motorcyclist arrived with another film, he was greeted cordially, which I think he appreciated.

Five

Prison Officers' Dispute

Yet another dispute which involved the Police, but was not caused by us. There was a work to rule by prison officers, I was not aware of everything the prison officers wanted, but I know we had to house prisoners in police cells, and the Home Office was footing the bill for the police overtime.

Police officers volunteered for this duty; they were offering to work on their rest days, but the gratuity was good for them, being a rest day they were paid time and a half, it was worth losing your rest day for. I was selected to help organise the running of the cell block, which included working out and selecting officers for respective duties. Each officer sent me a list of their rest days, showing whether they wanted to work a day shift or a night shift. I was inundated with notes from officers, which I put onto the duty rosters for each week. Once I had completed the list of duties, which officer was working which duty, the list was sent by telex to all the stations in the division, it usually arrived on a Wednesday. It was not unusual for officers to keep checking to see if the telex had arrived. One of the officers always assisted me with the task that had to be completed before the prisoners arrived, this included putting together the metal beds that were to be used, there were two beds to a cell, which meant we were accommodating twice as many prisoners than we should. We also hired a television from a local store, along with a video machine. Sheets and blankets had to be allocated to each of the cells, they were changed once a week, there were also pillows and towels, you would be surprised how little some prisoners possessed. We had to organise the meals from a local hotel, the bill for that was sent to me, I had a float to pay all the bills, I remember it was quite a large amount. There was a sergeant who had overall charge of the cellblock, he was a good friend of mine, we worked well together, and for most of the time, everything ran smoothly. Even though the life for our prisoners was a lot better than being in prison, there were still complaints. I think we came to realise that a few of our inmates lacked intelligence, they complained because there was nothing else to do.

We had a large car park at the rear of the station, we were able to use that to exercise the prisoners, once in the morning, and once in the afternoon. When the weather was fine the exercise was appreciated, it was also their right to exercise.

Our first consignment of prisoners came from the Metropolitan Police, they were from London courts, all these prisoners were remanded in custody until their next court date, they were, of course, innocent men, until the court convicted them of their offences. Once the prisoners arrived with us, so did the paperwork, their previous convictions were shown, it gave us an idea as to who we were dealing with, which was useful in some cases. It was quite usual for these prisoners to arrive after midnight, I think it was because they picked up at different courts in the capital, that took a lot of time. There were several of our inmates remanded for failing to pay the Poll Tax, a subject that was causing problems throughout the country. On arrival at the station, we went through the same procedure, booking everyone into a cell, checking on their dietary needs, then contacting the doctor to call in the following day. The doctor we had was an ex-Army doctor, he had heard all the tricks before, he was not going to be an easy touch, they all said they needed medication to sleep, this was a drug they used in the prison system. Our doctor did not prescribe any such drugs, he told them to take an aspirin before going to bed. Many of them were disappointed with the doctor, he could not be manipulated by the prisoners, he had dealt with soldiers, people who rarely complained about ailments, he was too much for the prisoners. Those who had been prescribed certain drugs, they were taken in the presence of a police officer, if not they saved them up, when they had a few they took them then, the prisoners were not trusted to take the drug as prescribed, so we looked over them like children. Some asked to see the doctor because they still could not sleep, once they were told it was going to be the same doctor, they changed their mind, the asprin seemed to be working.

Most of those were well behaved, they understood the job we were doing, but there are always exceptions to any rule, no matter how well you treat people.

One man who was on remand with us was a well-built man, who appeared to know his way around the criminal world, he was not only respected by the others, but they actually feared him, we decided to use this to our advantage. I was not sure where the fear lay, he was certainly big enough to look after himself, but I think he had influence outside the prison, a bit like the Krays when they were inside. We decided to have a quiet chat with him, trying to make sure there was no trouble from the other prisoners, he agreed to our terms, he did not want much. We delivered his meal first, making sure it was hot, that was really all he wanted, he accepted the cells were better than being in prison. He wanted to stay with us for as long as possible, he did not want any disruption in his new home. He told us he would keep everyone in order, he was as good as his word.

After several batches of prisoners from the Met, we were sent prisoners from the Bristol area, they were something of a surprise. They were all very young, being in prison was a completely new concept to them, the fact that they did not have to get up for work, they understood that. Looking at them I doubted any of them had done a day's work, that came across in their general behaviour. Not that they were a problem in the physical sense, they just moaned all the time. It was a bit like looking after a Kindergarten, except the children were brighter. None of these had committed anything serious, it was petty stuff, but they had continually floated the law. To them it was like an adventure, I think it helped to have people of the same age, they did not realise they were a short step away from prison, but I think they were soon to find out the realisation of their mistakes, and they would pay for those mistakes. Fortunately, they did not stay too long, we were glad to see them go, perhaps now we could get some adults, we got bored with the children. One of the children decided to barricade himself into his cell, but we did not panic, he came out because he was hungry, it was not a planned operation.

The next batch were certainly men, many of them violent, but they did not know any better, they were from Manchester. They were originally housed in Strangeways, it was a prison I thought to be tough, some of these prisoners showed that to be so, but they were alright. There was a couple of them that proved a nuisance, they were separated from the others. Several of these prisoners were accused of murder, several other for Grevious Bodily Harm, they were not a pleasant bunch as far as their offences were concerned, nobody was in for simple theft, all the offences appear to have violence attached. We decided to get one of the inmates on our side, a kind of informant, we found one man who said he would help, provided we looked after him. We agreed with looking after him, what we gave him I cannot remember, it was quite minor, but it meant a lot to him. He told me stories about his days on the streets in Manchester, he was part of a gang and had been shot twice, he showed me the scars, but I had no idea if they were the result of being shot, but I pretended I believed his tale. I was sure, if the tales were true, he was not someone who was going to live a full life, the cards were stacked against him.

One of the two men who had been separated was a very fat man, it is alleged he owned a classy nightclub in Manchester, which I was not too sure about, until he had a couple of visitors one evening. Two very attractive young ladies turned up, they were well-spoken and dressed expensively, they worked for the fat man, in his club. It was not only amazing how they looked, but it was who they were visiting, and they had travelled about 200 miles from Manchester, it is surprising what money can buy you.

Two of the Manchester inmates had been charged with rape, we had a whiteboard on which the prisoners' names were written, next to it was the offence each had been charged with, we decided to speak to these two and told them it would be theft on the board. The board could be seen by the prisoners, so we had to change it, it proved useful to us, those two prisoners were quiet throughout their stay.

Our informant informed us about the club the fat man owned, or part-owned as I was reliably informed, it was a very violent club, the fat man had a gang of minders taking care of him. It is a strange set of circumstances with the fat man having minders, I doubt any of them even liked him, it was the money that drove them to the job, something else you can buy with money. The fat man was someone who thought he was important in his neck of the woods, if he was the people around him were not very bright. He probably got the job because of his bulk, he did not appear to be bright enough to run a nightclub. The fat man had another man with him, although he was in the next cell, he was quite short, I think the fat man looked after him. The short man appeared to be lost without his partner, I cannot remember the fight they were involved in, but it was necessary to separate them from the rest of the prisoners.

Another man with the Manchester crowd was a Scotsman, he had obviously drifted away from home to commit his crimes. His convictions showed he had committed a great deal of crime In Manchester. He was someone who kept to himself, although he had the look of a man who could take care of himself. He never got involved in anything that was happening in the cell block, be it the television or video, he remained in his cell and read, he was no trouble to us.

At visiting time there were not many visitors, at the most three, they all wanted to see the fat man. It was a pleasant sight for the officers on duty, mini-skirted young ladies, all with long legs and dressed to kill. I enjoyed their visits, as did all the other officers, they came in every day, always dressed in different clothes. I cannot be sure if they had come from Manchester each day, or it is more likely they found accommodation in the area. It seems the rest of the prisoners had no friends, or the journey from Manchester was too long and too expensive. All the prisoners wanted to go back to Manchester, even Strangeways appealed to them, but they were stuck with us for the foreseeable future. They returned to Manchester when they were due to appear in court. I cannot remember how long they stayed, it was about three weeks I believe, they were pleased to be leaving, apart from the girls, we were pleased to see them go.

Our next intake was from London, yet again, they arrived and left at regular intervals, they were not a problem, although most were in for serious offences. I think probably it was because they did not stay too long, there was not enough time to get bored. The main disadvantage was the time of their arrival, usually in the early hours of the morning, they sometimes departed at that time as well, it prevented the escorts making two trips. The ardent criminal liked staying at the police station, he got more freedom than he got in prison. We had a couple of prisoners causing a problem, but they were the sort to cause a problem in an empty room, it necessitated those individuals being moved, away from the general populace, they were moved next door, in what we called the solitary confinement cells. Some of the prisoners liked being in solitary, but I do not believe those prisoners had any friends, to them it was a normal life, living alone with nobody to talk to. I actually know people like that, they are quite boring because they have no interests. Most of the clients we had from the Met, were being dealt with at Horseferry Road Magistrates, not that it makes a lot of difference, but that court was very busy. I think it was a strict court, not well-liked by prisoners, mainly because they locked them up, rather than releasing them on the community.

The prisoners from London liked being in our cells, particularly those who had tasted prison proper.

There were several prisoners who we took note of, one was in for rape for the second time, although we never advertised this fact, perhaps we should have. Some of the other prisoners appeared to recognise him, he had recently been released from prison for his first rape, then off he goes and commits another rape, he obviously had a problem. His big problem was that he could not get a girlfriend, if that was the case, why not go to a prostitute, that would save him the long sentence. I cannot remember what his sentence was for the first rape, but the second rape in such a short time after leaving prison, he was looking at a big sentence, possibly life. He was a very quiet man, not the sort that had the potential to be a rapist, but keeping low may have been his way of avoiding contact with other prisoners, particularly if someone recognised him. I never knew what happened to him in court, hopefully, he got what he deserved.

Three other prisoners were in for not paying Poll Tax, that was something everybody understood, they were not real criminals, just normal guys. We thought being incarcerated with us was probably a frightening experience. It seemed unfair that they should share the cell block with real criminals, but that was how the law worked. We got one of them to leave the cellblock and make the tea for the prisoners, it was felt he was unlikely to try for an escape, which he did not, he also did a good job of making the tea,

The next person was an armed robber, he had in fact committed several robberies, he said it was never his intention to harm anyone, the gun he had was never loaded. I said that the person he pointed it at, was not aware the weapon was not loaded, in fact, quite the opposite, they thought it was loaded. He eventually saw my point of view, but I doubted that would make him change his ways, I still expected him to commit armed robberies until the sentences reflected how scared he had made people.

Another prisoner was more than a little confused with his situation, he did not know where he was, or why he was there, the doctor examined him and thought he was as sane as I was. I did not like the doctor referring to me in that way, particularly if at a later stage the prisoner was deemed to be insane. This particular prisoner never ventured outside his cell, he refused exercise, never watched the television, and he never spoke to other inmates. We kept an eye on him, but we thought he was trying to pull a fast one, but why would anyone want to go to a mental institution, I appreciate the sentence might be easier, but you had to leave at some time. This man seemed the ideal candidate to commit suicide, he shared a cell with another inmate, we shared our worries with him, he said he hardly spoke, but he would keep an eye on him. My sergeant was concerned about him, so he rang the Met to share his concerns, they turned up the following and took him back to the capital, they believed they were better equipped to look after him.

We had several prisoners that one could class as well educated, they were in for fraud or similar, they were not violent men, they used their brains rather than their brawn. Even well-educated men get caught, they thought they could outsmart the system, that did not work, and now they had to pay for that mistake. They occasionally talked when on their exercise period, they did not divulge any of their secrets, I think they thought about how they get caught, they did not intend to make the same mistakes when they tried again. They were interesting, but they gave nothing away, I wonder where they are now, possibly running the country.

The next man was very special, he lived in his own little bubble, convincing himself that the things he was saying were true, except his world was all fantasy. He reminded me of the Indian gentleman I mentioned earlier, the one that needed four CID officers to arrest him. He kept talking about the operation he had been on, which he could not talk about because he was working for the government. For someone who could not talk about it, he had a lot to say. When asked if he had ever killed anyone, he said he had not, the minnows in the operation did all that, he was a senior man and did not get his hands dirty. His crimes went back a bit, he was involved in the assassination of President Kennedy, that was two people I knew who were involved in that, he was not put off when I mentioned he was only two years old at the time, he quickly moved on. He did ask that the Home Secretary was informed of his whereabouts, just like the Indian man, I wondered how many agents the Home Secretary had in the field, when you consider there were two in Amersham.

The next inmate was a very angry young man, he felt the world owed him something, although he did not have a job, he still felt he was owed something. Following a couple of minor punch ups in the cell block, he was moved into a cell on his own, the door remained lock, it was only opened to allow him to take exercise. He was moved to protect himself, someone in the cell block would have done him serious injury if he had remained there. He was glad of the exercise, he had quietened down, he did not like being locked in his cell, it was up to him to change his ways, which I thought he might have understood. Following a few of these exercise periods, he asked if he could be returned to the cell bloke, promising to stop his violence towards other inmates, he seemed genuine so we let him return. To start with we kept a close eye on him, he appeared to be behaving, he was even talking to other inmates, he had never done that before. There was never any need to segregate him again, he had learnt a lesson, and to be honest, so had we, segregation was good for those failing to conform. Our man continued to behave himself, right up until he was returned to the Met.

Most of the prisoners were old-timers, they appreciated they were well off in police cells, they did not want to rock the boat, they behaved. It was our job to let everyone know about the rules that were laid down, if the youngsters did not like it, I felt sure the older inmates would let them know how to behave.

There was one rule the prisoners did not like, but it was one they had to accept. On each visit an officer sat in, he was ensuring nothing was being passed to the prisoner. All the officers took their turn on the visits, on some occasions, it was not such an inconvenience, particularly if the visitor was a beautiful female, just like the fat man's visitors. What is the reason attractive women are attracted to criminals, it must be the excitement, but our prisoners were not that exciting, they had been caught. It was not because the prisoners were good looking, in most cases they were far from that, I think the prisoners told these girls stories of their exploits, not necessarily true stories, but enough to excite the girls. There were a number of prisoners who never had a visitor at all, this was understandable for the Manchester prisoners, but we were on the underground, so there should not have been a problem travelling from London. It was possible that many of the London prisoners had spent most of their lives behind bars, maybe their families had given up with them, wiped them out of their lives, that could be the same with the youngsters. It was strange listening into conversations with their girlfriends, it was all about having a holiday when they got out, sometimes to exotic places, bearing in mind the prisoner was not only out of work, but had been for years. It sounded like another offence of theft or burglary was going to pay for these holidays. I know not many made these trips, it was a way of thinking ahead, it was a way of getting rid of negativity, I have no idea if it worked or not. It did not matter if the evidence against them was overwhelming, they still felt the court was going to release them. I appreciate they needed something to aim for, but if they were guilty and they knew it, why did they not see a prison sentence at the end of the trial, I think optimism sometimes went a bit too far. It was interesting the tales they told each other, the favourite was they had been fitted up by the police, this was a recurring theme, I often wondered if it was the same policeman. The wives and girlfriends sat there and listened, the older ones had heard it all before, in fact, every time he went in prison, some of these prisoners had been fitted up as many as ten times. The younger wives and girlfriends listened intently, concerned that the police carried out such practices, I was concerned by these practices, I have no idea where these practices were carried out. I think the ladies were just doing their duty, listening to the ravings of their menfolk. I did not, for obvious reasons, attend any of the court dates, so I have no idea how the men reacted in court. I have been to court many times, I have never heard a prisoner tell the court he was fitted up, if they had I am sure the court would ask him to explain what that meant, followed by an enquiry into the officer's conduct. Talking away from the court, is exactly that, just talk, it is something you tell your girlfriend. I think the media is partly to blame, maybe they started using the term. To return to the story, I think I know why these prisoners believe they were fitted up, they have said it enough to fellow prisoners, they start believing it. It is strange that every prisoner in prison is innocent, that being the case there are a lot of guilty men walking the streets. It would be nice to hear someone in prison admit to committing the crime. Not many of the prisoners liked the police, that was mainly because they put them behind bars, it did not matter that they committed the crime, they did not like being caught, and committing the crime was not their fault, how could we think that.

We never checked to see how these prisoners got on in court, we were too busy for that, and to be honest, we were not really that interested, we were getting new prisoners daily.

The only prisoner I showed interest in was the rapist, as with all rapists, I hope he got what he deserved, but that would never be enough.

When the Met brought us new prisoners, they sometimes brought us reports on who was likely to cause us trouble, it was useful to get, we normally kept a close eye on them. The troublemakers were passed from police station to police station, sometimes hundreds of miles apart, but usually the real troublemakers were accepted back into the prison system. It was not that we could not handle them, it was just our handling of them may not conform to prison methods, causing the prisoner to make a complaint, it did not take much for some of the prisoners to complain. The system was that these type of prisoners were housed in prison, in an environment they understood, most of them had spent the majority of their life behind bars, they understood the system quite easily. They knew when it was mealtime, when they got their exercise, when it was time for visitors, if they got any. All this they understood, being housed in a police station they could not get to grips with. These prisoners could see their lives out in prison, provided everything stayed the same.

There is one further story to tell before we finish, that is prisoners who barricade themselves in cells, we know they are attention-seeking, but one of ours damaged stuff inside the cell. We used the ancient trick of ignoring him, he would come out when he became hungry, he stuck it for most of the day, then he asked if he could have his meal in the cell, this was of course refused. Once he had come out someone went into the cell to check on the damage he had caused, there was quite a bit of damage. Once he had finished his meal he was taken to a room, there he was charged with the damage he had caused, this shocked him, he did not realise he was going to be charged, because the damage was caused inside the police station. Strange how some people think, but then he did have the mentality of a dormouse.

Six

I will now move onto other situations I have either dealt with or been part of the team dealing with certain incidents.

The first was a situation that occurred in Beaconsfield. There was a man up a tree with a rope around his neck, sounded like he was about to commit suicide, we were sent there. He was in a wooded area near some houses, he was a young man who was talking to CID officers when we attended. The two of us were told to get behind a tree, about 20 yards from the man in the tree, the CID was concerned in case he made a break for it, although it was unknown at this stage what he had done. We could hear CID talking to him, they were trying hard to find out why he was in the tree, but he would not say, then he suddenly decided to open up. He told CID that he had killed someone, they asked him the necessary questions, who was he it he had killed, I think he said his landlord. He gave the address, then he threw them the front door key, this had to be checked out as a matter of urgency, sending a uniform officer to the address. He came back and reported there was a dead man in the lounge, he had been stabbed, these details were passed over the radio, then someone in the control room asked if the rest of the house had been checked out. The rest of the house had not been checked out, someone was dispatched there to check the upstairs of the house, there they found a female stabbed to death, but that was not all. Another officer checked the outhouse, to his surprise he found the body of their teenage son, he had also been stabbed, we now had a triple murder, and the culprit was stuck in a tree. While this was going on a member of the press went to a nearby house and offered the lady £1,000 to take a photograph of the man, he wanted to take it from her bedroom window, which had a good view of the tree, I refused him permission, which he grudgingly accepted. I left the scene at 10 pm, the man was still in the tree, and CID was still talking to him, one of them told him to jump, it would save time and money. I went home and turned up the following morning on early turn, I was told to go to the cell block, I did not expect the prisoner to be the one from the previous night, there was already an officer looking after him, but during the night the prisoner had made a worrying remark. He had asked the officer if his sentence would be any larger if he killed the officer, bearing in mind the prisoner was a powerfully built man, I understood why my colleague was concerned, particularly as the prisoner was not confined to his cell. The only thing I remember he talked about was whether the press was outside the station, I thought maybe he wanted to carry out a press conference, I think he would have agreed to that if it was offered, it was not offered. We took him to court that morning, the court was at the end of an underground tunnel, which he looked at, before realising there was no means of escape. Once in court he said nothing, he did not even confirm his name, the magistrates had little choice, they remanded him in custody until his Crown Court hearing, it was only a Crown Court who could hand out the sentence he deserved. I later found out he was sent to Broadmoor for an indefinite period, how long that is I do not know, he might still be there, but I expect the do-gooders got him released, so he could carry out more murders.

Another incident I dealt with was a bit strange, although a little entertaining. It involved an enquiry from the Metropolitan Police, they wanted me to interview a lady about an accident she was involved in, this enquiry was bigger than both of us, I will start by saying she was young and attractive, but there was more to her than that. She remembered the incident I was referring to, but this was no ordinary traffic accident. I asked her to explain what had happened, then the fictitious series of events started. She said she was chased across London by two men in a car, she had no idea why they were chasing her, she did try to explain that, but it was very confused. She reached a large hotel during the chase, left her car outside and went into the hotel, there she booked into a room, she went to her room but did not stop, she left the hotel and drove off in her car. I asked her about the accident she was involved in, she denied even being involved in an accident. There were two choices her, she was either lying, or her head was playing tricks on her, I believed it to be the second option. There was no doubt in my mind this lady was crazy, I doubted the story about the hotel ever happened, I understood why the Met had passed it onto us, I expect they were delighted when they found out she lived in our area. I repeated the allegations against her several times, but on each occasion she denied it. I then reported her for the traffic offence, I had little choice. I sent the paperwork back to the Met, along with my thoughts on the case, I never heard anymore, I did not even get a court warning. It seems likely the case was dropped because of the mental state of the lady.

I carried out an enquiry for the City of London Police, it was the only enquiry I ever got from them. I interviewed and reported the gentleman, as I was requested, I returned the enquiry, I thought no more about it. Sometime later I had a court warning for the Mansion House Court in the City of London, I had never given evidence at this court, nor had any of my colleagues, it was going to be an experience. I got to the court to be greeted by the WPC who was the officer in the case, she had sent me the original enquiry, what she told me surprised me, she was prosecuting the case, no barristers or solicitors, she was doing the questioning. It was something they carried out in the City, they prosecuted their own cases, which I thought from an experience point of view, it was a terrific idea. I got into the witness box and swore the oath, then she questioned me, before moving onto the defence solicitor, I think she won the case. It was something I never forgot, for officers to prosecute their own cases, the system must have had confidence in them, the WPC who questioned me was very good, she did not leave any details outstanding.

As I say it was the only time I gave evidence in the City, I was not aware of other forces prosecuting their own cases, maybe it was because they were not that busy, that was a possibility but very unlikely. It certainly proved to be a good system, the officers would learn from the experience, it would also free up solicitors, I liked the idea.

I have come across several well-known people in my police experiences, the first was Barbera Windsor, or should I say Dame.

Barbera Windsor, she owned a public house just outside Amersham. It was November the 5th, there was an organised bonfire near her pub, myself and a colleague attended, knowing there was fire present it might prove too much for the local delinquents. She greeted us when we arrived, bringing us tea before the fireworks started, many people thought Miss Windsor was far from polite towards the police, we did not find that. Once the fireworks had finished she actually came out and thanked us for being there, not something that was done by someone who was not polite. A colleague of mine was suspicious of her when she arrived at the pub, he was convinced the hard men of the East End would turn up in their droves. He checked a few cars that turned up, they were all innocent, after a short while he gave it up, but he did occasionally return and check out the cars.

There is someone else I want to mention, he was a friend of mine who lived in Amersham Old Town, he ran the local auction as well as having a shop in the town. His name was Martin and he was known by everyone in Amersham, he was enthusiastic about buying antiques, providing the price was right, his price was usually completely different from the items true value. I did on occasion listen to Martin talking to a customer, it was certainly entertaining. If a piece of furniture was brought in, Martin looked it over, then he offered the seller £15, which occasionally showed shock on the face of the seller, with good reason. If the seller wanted more, that was where negotiations broke down. If the seller accepted his price, the money was handed over and the piece of furniture was priced up at £25, it was a cash transaction, I do not think anything went through the books. He remained in the shop for many years, carrying out the auctions on a Saturday, then came the time when he had to sell the shop, he owed money to all the official organisations, VAT was not paid, he did not pay Income Tax, mainly because nobody knew what he earned, I doubt that he did. This was the problem with all his cash transactions, he lost track of who he owed. I was sorry to see him sell his shop, but he had brought it on himself. He eventually sold the business and moved to Australia with his new wife, I wonder what they thought of him down under.

There was another minor incident that happened, I was driving an unmarked police car from Gerrards Cross to Amersham, in the passenger seat was Sue, she was the secretary in our office at Gerrards Cross. We had come to a halt in the road, a car three cars in front of us wanted to turn right, we waited patiently, then I saw a car approaching from behind us, it appeared to be going too fast to stop. I told Sue to prepare for a collision, which she did. The car hit us and pushed us forward into the two cars in front, I got out as did the offending driver, he apologised and said he would give us his insurance, but he realised I was a police officer and I told him this was a police vehicle. I think he cursed under his breath. I contacted the control room and asked that a traffic sergeant attend. The sergeant turned up and dealt with it, my vehicle was taken in for repair, the back was well damaged, the front was a little.

There was a gentleman in Amersham Old Town who I occasionally visited, I found out from his wife he was an Austrian Prince, not the sort of prince you bow to, more an honorary title. Both were very polite and pleased to see me, they went to Austria a couple of times a year, particularly at Christmas, when they returned they took in two tins of biscuits, to thank the police for looking after their house. Nobody at the police station knew anything about it, I was the one checking out their house, in saying that the biscuits soon disappeared. I also went and thanked them for the biscuits, although others in the station had a lot more than I did.

I did on occasion visit the local Primary School to give a talk, it was more the younger age group, talking about Stranger Danger, it was to discourage them from talking to someone they did not know. I felt sure the teachers had done it before me, but maybe someone in uniform had some impact. I enjoyed the school talks, but it was when I asked if there were any questions that things started to change. Small children have wonderful imaginations, they can easily take another track. The questions varied between someone seeing a burglar the previous night, once one of the children said that the rest joined in, they had all seen a burglar had some time, or a robber, that was their favourite.

The Committee for the Amersham Town Half Marathon.
I am number 516, with the hand of Barbera Windsor on my right shoulder and Debbie Curtis's hand on my left shoulder.

To add to something already mentioned, Martin was on the committee for the Amersham Town Half Marathon, and Barbera Windsor was good enough to start the race, we appreciated what both of them had done.

Another celebrity I met was Michael Dennison, I was dealing with a collision for the Metropolitan Police, he was involved, so I needed to go and see him.

I went to his flat on the Shadaloes Estate in Amersham, he was on the ground floor, and was very welcoming. He knew what the enquiry was about, about from ageing a little, I recognised him instantly, his voice was very distinctive from his acting days. On my visit a colleague asked if I could get an autograph from Dulcie Gray, which was, of course, Michael Dennison's wife, she was charming and was happy to sign a photograph for me. I carried out the interview successfully, and I was served tea by the great Dulcie Gray. I sat in the flat looking around, a bit nosey really, but I wanted to see if there was any memorabilia from his film, I could not see anything, I decided it was rude to ask. What I did notice was the piles of newspapers in the corners of the room, I am not talking a few newspapers, these piles were about two foot high. I assumed they had some connection with their acting, I believe Dulcie Gray at the time was on stage at Windsor. On the large piano, at least that was how I remember it, was a large signed photograph of the Queen Mother, I asked about it. I was told that she visited on occasions, no doubt top security was the order of the day. We were never told about her visits at the police station, why should we be, it was very hush-hush, not for the likes of us flat foots. I never found out the result of the case, I never saw Michael Dennison again, I believe he passed away a short time later, but he was a very nice man. There are other people I will mention during this tale, one such man was Roy Castle. He was visiting a local school, no doubt for some charitable cause, two of went along to make sure he was kept safe. He chatted to the children for some time, then he came outside, again we spoke to a lovely man. I was sad to hear he had passed away, I believe it was cancer, yet he had a healthy lifestyle and never smoked.

One incident occurred which made me feel ashamed. I was well in with many of the local shopkeepers in Amersham Old Town, one of them approached me one day, he said he had received information that his shop was going to be broken into before Christmas, this was a week before Christmas. The only way into his shop was by going in the back way, this was near the rear of the hotel. It was decided this was the only way in, the front of the shop was on the high street. I informed control that I would be watching the rear of the premises all night, they would hear from me if a vehicle came in the back way. I positioned myself up a small tree, giving me all-round views, but I was able to see the back of the shop clearly, which was the main objective of the operation. It was a long night when there was nothing happening, but I felt it was worthwhile if we caught some burglars. The shop itself was an expensive food shop, at that time of year it was full of poultry and game birds, very valuable, it also possessed all the luxury items going with the game birds. The first night passed quietly, nobody asked if I was alright, I had contacted the control room at the beginning of the shift, and again when I was clocking off, I heard nothing from anyone else. The second, third, and fourth nights were still quiet, then came my last night, the 22nd December, but that did not stir me in any way, it was still quiet. The following day was December 23rd, which was an ideal day for the theft, it left a day before Christmas to get rid of the stock. I said I was happy to work that night, although it was my rest day, it seemed sensible to reallocate the rest day, but the inspector decided there was no need. He said the shift would keep an eye on it overnight, which did not fill me with too much joy. On occasions like this, the shift do not bother to look in on places, I was concerned but the inspector would not budge.

I came to work the following morning to find out the shop had been burgled overnight, to say I was annoyed was an understatement. The inspector was not at work, so I went and saw the superintendent, to let off my rage at a stupid decision made by the inspector, perhaps he could go and see the shop owner, who lost £30,000 worth of goods. The superintendent listened to what I had to say, but it was unlikely he would mention it to the inspector. Once again we have senior officers who are completely useless, there was never an apology from the inspector, and I had to face the shop owner and apologise for the dregs of humanity that served in the police. It saddens me that I put a lot of work into that observation, but others do not care, whether the night shift checked the shop is unlikely, if future tales are right, which I will explain after this. Just after that, I packed in my area beat in Amersham Old Town, partly because I was embarrassed to see the shop owner, not that it was my fault, but the embarrassment was for the shift that could not be bothered.

I am not sure it was the same shift, but this story is hard to believe. In Amersham there was a library bus parked up, I believe outside the library, the most logical place, it was left there overnight. We turned up for briefing to be told the library bus had been stolen the previous night, when it happened we did not know, that was until an officer piped up, he had seen the bus the previous night. When questioned as to what time he saw it, he was quick to answer about 4 am, the obvious question was asked as to why he did not stop it, did he think people were changing library books at that hour. I believe the library bus was recovered, unlikely you could drive it around, unless a particular shift were on duty, then it would be alright.

Another snippet involves details of a new warrant card that was to be issued to officers, I am not sure if they wanted suggestions, or maybe they were just telling us, either way, I thought they wanted suggestions for the make-up of the new card. I put a report in and suggested the new card should have the officer's blood group on it, it would assist medical staff in case the officer was involved in an accident. Not only did I not get a response, but my suggestion was obviously not considered, not because it was a bad suggestion, but I was not senior enough to make such a suggestion.

There was a new Tesco store opening in Old Amersham, I met the security men there, they were very friendly and often invited me in for a tea, in their staff canteen. Once it was open there was a night shift working there, I think they were the shelf fillers, preparing for trading the following day, there were a few people working there that I knew in a professional way, but the security staff already knew about them. I cannot remember exactly when the store opened, but I went down there just before Christmas, the manager invited me and the shift for a Christmas Dinner, but this was not during the day. We were working a night shift, as were the staff in the shop, but there was one problem, the inspector would not hear of it. It was the same inspector who was involved in the shop burglary, shame he could not take other parts of the job more serious. I think there were eight on the shift, so we worked it out that the officers could attend in two lots of four, once one left the other four turned up, it kept officers on the street. The inspector was not invited, rather than tell him and get ourselves banned, we decided to say nothing, I do not think he ever knew what went on. The meal itself was excellent, although the Christmas pudding was a bit heavy on the stomach when I got home at 6 am, we thanked our hosts for their kindness, it was a lovely gesture. The following Christmas I had moved away from Amersham, but I still remember that Christmas early lunch, and the fact the inspector was not invited, he did not deserve to be, remembering his mistakes, which cost one particular person a lot of money.

There were several people in the police I did not like too much, but there was a lot I liked and trusted.

While still on the subject of Christmas, there is another interesting tale, it took place on Christmas Eve, in Chesham. We had been told about a burglary taking place in a local school, we made our way there, locating ourselves on the perimeter of the school, I waited by a bush, which was much taller than the car. Suddenly there was a noise as someone vaulted over the fence, to his surprise I was stood only a few feet away.

"What have you been up to?" I said.

"Nothing," he said.

It was not an original reply, so I arrested him on suspicion of burglary, to which he said, I remember it clearly.

"But it's Christmas," he said.

"Have you been doing some Christmas shopping?" I said.

To my surprise he had no goods on him, he thought that put him in the clear, but his friends were caught with the goods, saying he was there. What a shame they did not leave him out of it, but they are criminals, it was unlikely that they wanted to take all the blame. This was another house we had to search on Christmas Day, it was not exactly dressed in festive attire. Why do people who are married to criminals, not too concerned when he fails to come home for Christmas. I guess she knew he was going to commit a burglary with his friends, him not coming home told her that he had not been successful. I find it strange that the burglary was committed on Christmas Eve, there are other days leading up to Christmas, but they left it to the last moment, that meant one thing, they would spend Christmas Day in the cell. The man who I arrested had a couple of young children, he was obviously not too worried about them, perhaps all their Christmases had been spent without their father, I think on this occasion he was looking at a long sentence.

One other little event which was suffered by all sergeants, that was the pub checks, the sergeant was accompanied by another officer, why that was never got explained to me. The sergeant and I visited several pubs in Amersham Old Town, I knew the landlords and their staff. It was one of the staff from one of the pubs that made my sergeant take a step back, I introduced him but he was still nervous of shaking hands with this man, I think the dress frightened him a bit, the moustache did not help his outfit. I cannot remember the man's name, but he was well known about the town, it just showed how much the sergeant went out, if he had he might have come across him. My sergeant did not get over the experience, he asked me on other visits, was there anything I needed to tell him, but that was the only man dressed as a woman. He certainly attracted the punters, that pub was usually full, but he was also a very good barman, treated everyone the same, even my sergeant.

There was another interesting incident that happened on my patch, jewellers in the Old Town had a silver jug brought in, he was a bit suspicious of the two men that brought it in, he rang me and asked me to pop in. I went in and examined the jug, which made me even more suspicious, it had a name engraved on it, it was a surname I recognised. I asked the jeweller if I could take the jug to show it to someone who might know a bit more about it, he agreed. I only had to walk a short distance in the Old Town, to see the boyfriend of Miss Debbie Curtis, she is mentioned in one of the running photographs, he had a very unusual surname, which happened to be engraved on the jug. When I showed him the jug he was delighted, saying that it had been stolen from his father's house, the name related to his father, the theft had taken place some twenty years previously. We now knew who the owner was, it was now the son who owned it, where it had been stolen from, it was in a burglary, nobody was ever found for the offence. I was not sure we were going to get the actual burglars, but I felt there was a story that needed to be told, I was ready to listen, as was the magistrates. We asked the jewellery shop owner what was his agreement with the person who brought it in, they simply wanted it valued. I asked the owner if he could telephone them and ask them to come in. He did have details of the car they were driving, which helped immensely during the operation. He rang the man and asked him to come in, there was a day and time arranged. This operation involved the whole shift, I was in the shop, but in the back room, the car was spotted going past the shop and parking up. Two men came into the shop, the owner walked to the back room, I walked out to confront them, my colleague walked in the door to stop their exit. I did not know it at the time, but a WPC colleague arrested the lady who was driving the car, I arrested both men, we then took them to the police station. They appeared too young to have been involved in the original burglary, there was much more to this story. They were not too concerned about being arrested, in fact, I think they expected it. I interviewed the first man who admitted the jug was stolen, but not from many years ago, he had stolen it only a few days before, from a lady who owed him money. I believe, from what he told me, the lady was renting his flat, the trouble was she did not pay any rent. When she was leaving the flat she packed up all her furniture, putting it in a trailer attached to her car, that was when our man struck, he took the jug from the trailer. He did not think it was really theft, he was getting back something that was owed, but he admitted to it once the police were involved, but not the theft I was concerned with. I asked him the details of the lady in question, which he was happy to give me, but her address was unknown, seeing as he had just thrown her out. I had details of the trailer and used that to look around the town, but there was no sign of her or the trailer. It appears that the description given by the man, was unlikely to fit that of a person who had committed the burglary over twenty years ago, but I thought she might have some information on the offender, possibly her father or mother. It seemed I was unlikely to know, all my enquiries reached a dead end. I went up to CID to pass on the information I had, along with the lady's name, they were interested until I said she had disappeared, they gave me their tale of woe. The lady in question was one of a team of burglars, CID had been looking for them for months, but no luck, this did not help telling them she had just moved. The jug was returned to the rightful owner, he was very pleased with that, we never heard any more of the lady who was a burglar, nor any of her associates. I was still concerned about the jug, I do not think it had any real value, only sentimental to the family, which I saw it was of value to them. The big question was where had it been for twenty years, how many hands did it pass through? It was a question I wished I had answered, the owner of the jug asked me those questions, but I could not answer them, it had obviously been hidden away somewhere, how did the young lady get her hands on it? It was one of those problems which you would have loved to have found out, but the young lady only had part of the story. As far as the two men I arrested were concerned, they were not charged with theft, had they tried to sell the jug it would have been a different matter, but they only wanted a valuation. The jug was returned to the rightful owner. I would have liked to have found out more, but sometimes these problems would never be solved.

There was a young officer at Amersham, he was a probationer, I think he had only been in a couple of months, when he suddenly decided to leave. It appears he had won a house, I believe in the north of England, he had entered a competition in the newspaper and won the first prize. Several senior officers tried to talk him out of leaving, but his mind was made up. I do not think he was married, so there was only himself to think about, he did show everyone a photograph of the house, it did look delightful. He worked out his notice then he left, he did not have a job to go to, but he had a house with no mortgage, this seemed to cover his lack of employment. We never heard from him again, no doubt he was living out his life in his house. You occasionally come across people like that, winners in the obstacle course of life, but they are few and far between, we all wished him good luck, although at this stage I have no idea of his name.

There is one man who I feel I should mention, he ran a haulage firm just outside Amersham, he was not easy to see, at least that was what the WPC in our department said. She was the lazy one who I think I mentioned earlier, he frightened her with his aggressive tone. When I moved into the department the areas had been moved prior to my arrival, I got the aggressive man, once the areas had been changed around to suit her. I did not know that at the time, but to be honest, it did not bother me, I wanted to do the job, she did not.

On my first visit there he was too busy to see me, I said I would wait, which I did for a short time, then he agreed to see me. I had many enquiries about his vehicles not being insured, which he agreed with me they were not, many because it was much too expensive to insure them, he would go out of business if he insured them all, so he insured a few at a time. The trouble was our traffic department knew about him, whenever they saw his vehicles they stopped him, then they should have reported him for the offence, but they did not, subsequently, I had to see him and report him. As my visits became more regular, he became a little more friendly towards me, he started to offer me cups of tea, this was indeed a revelation. I appreciate he should have insured all his vehicles, but it was very expensive to do so, I had some sympathy with him, unlike my colleagues who I had no sympathy for. I saw the gentleman later as he was leaving Aylesbury Crown Court, he shook hands with me and said hello. I have no idea how much he had been fined over the years, it was certainly in the thousands.

There was a person I had to see on a farm type building, it was to do with an accident. I looked around but there was nobody there, I thought I might be at the wrong premises. There were several cars at the back of the house, I checked the registration with our control room, both vehicles came back as stolen from Reading the previous day. I decided to look around the house again, there was a shed at the back, there were several men working in there, I asked where the owner was, they said he would be back soon. I then enquired as to who owned the cars, once again the owner was mentioned. I was there on my own so I asked for back up, particularly as the owner was likely to make a run for it when he saw me there. A few colleagues turned up, followed by the owner, who actually admit one of the stolen cars was his, a strange admission to make. My colleagues got some other officers to call in, there was another shed with three stolen vehicle in there, it was now a case for the stolen vehicle squad to deal with. I arrested the owner of the property for the one stolen vehicle, the other officer there made enquiries with the staff there, I believe another three people were arrested and five stolen vehicles were recovered. I cannot remember what happened to the car thieves, I was not asked to give evidence, I can only assume they pleaded guilty, I do not think they had much of a choice in the matter.

There is one officer who needs a special mention, he was one of the keenest officers on the station, both inside the station, and as it happens his skill outside was well known. If he was in the office as Station Duty Officer, there was no need to ask him to do things if he sent you to a job, he was carrying out these tasks as you attended. When the job was finished, he had already written the result on the paperwork, he was a wonderful addition to the shift, although not all shifts felt the same. When I went out onto the streets, it was reassuring to find him sat in the office, most people thought like that, the ones that did not were not out on the streets.

There were several incidents on the street involving him, the first was when he went out merely to go to the bank, before he returned there were numerous telephone calls, they all referred to this policeman directing the traffic. He should have been on his way back to the station, instead, he did not feel the traffic was moving efficiently enough, so he decided to lend a hand, whether that improved the flow I cannot remember. He returned to the station none the worst for his experience.

There was another more serious incident, he was actually on foot patrol in the town. He had reason to stop a car, the trouble was the driver did not want to stop, he was about to drive away when the officer jumped on the bonnet and hung on. The incident could have caused the officer serious injuries, but other patrols came to his assistance. The driver went to court and was severely punished for carrying an officer on his bonnet, I think after that he always stopped for the police.

There was another officer who had a strange phobia, she always fainted when in the witness box giving evidence. I feel sure she was not the only one, but it was the only one I knew of. She was put in the office as the duty officer, in theory, it stopped her giving evidence in court, I am not sure how successful this ploy was, I never remember her going to court.

There is one more story, or should I say it is the result of many stories that I heard at the Crown Court. The defendant was tried and found guilty of whatever offence he had been charged with, he then made his plea, or should I say his solicitor made his plea, not for him to be sent to prison. The peculiar situation arose in a great number of cases, particularly after the verdict had been given, The defendant did not want to go to prison, mainly because he was starting a new job on Monday, the fact that this defendant had not worked for over five years, it was a miracle he had found a job. I think this scenario turned up at least a dozen times in my experience. The judges knew the form, they rarely believed these people had a job.

Seven

In this chapter, I would like to discuss several courses I attended, along with my own indulgence into my sporting repertoire.

The first course was the Continuation Course, this was the final course of the probationary period, it normally took place after 18 months, it was a sort of confirmation that you had passed your probationary period.

The thing I liked about it was we were meeting up with the people I joined with, most of them had been sent to other stations within the force area, I, therefore, did not see them, this was an opportunity to catch up. One of our group was an ex-naval man, I got on well with him, we decided on the course to set him up, not for any other reason than we knew he would take it as a joke. We had cleared one of the classrooms, then we set it up as a court, he was about to be tried by his classmates, we had a prosecutor, a defence solicitor, and of course a judge. There was a new class at the centre, they were in their first week in the police, we persuaded them to act as the jury, which they were glad to do. Our victim was brought to court, although he had no idea what was happening, he thought we were going to the bar, he was shocked when he came into the classroom and found it all set up. He was charged with gross indecency, I believe a cow was mentioned, we went through the complete trial, he had a chance to speak at the end, he was speechless. The jury found him guilty and he was sentenced to imprisonment, then we went to the bar to celebrate the case, our colleague enjoyed himself in the box, although he did refuse to give evidence, that I believe was a sign of his guilt. Our instructor found out about the case, he was amused that we had got away with it. Perhaps it was some kind of omen, but in my police career, I dealt with many cases of gross indecency, was this case preparing me for what was to come, I think maybe it was.

The rest of the course was quite easy, I think it was accepted that we had all completed our probation successfully, it was, therefore, a relaxing week, plenty of football on the outside pitch. There were four girls in our class, they played as well, but they proved very violent, which surprised me with one of them, she was very petite. We enjoyed the bar facilities, taking advantage of it at every opportunity, which was every night, our classmate ran the bar he was very good and very cheap. I cannot think the force made much profit that week, I felt it was likely they lost money. Once the course was over we returned to our stations, many of those on the course, I would never see again, which was sad as it was a good course, but life moves on.

On returning to my station I was aware of a Half Marathon taking place in High Wycombe, strangely I volunteered to take part, which was strange as I had never run such a distance, it was representing a police team. I decided to train for the event, 13 miles was a long way, this was carried out daily, I waited for my rest days to run a long distance. It was only on the day of the race that I realised the obstacle that awaited us. The race started on the Rye, a nice piece of grass, then the race moved towards Marlow Hill, a very steep piece of the course. We had to go up the hill, which was steep enough to hurt your legs, the one advantage was the course was all downhill after Marlow Hill, by which time your legs are crying out. It was a slow run up the hill, many had decided to walk, I started to think was not a bad idea, but I kept running. I felt it was slower running up the hill, than if I had gone for a fast walk, but I did not walk, this gave me some satisfaction. On reaching the top I smiled to myself, I had got up the hill without walking, but my legs felt the exertion of the run, but it was all downhill from here. The trouble was there was still another 12 miles to complete the course, I set off full of hope.

The photograph shows the team before the start, we were optimistic, a little stupid maybe, but confident of completing the task. I did finish the race, my time was under

2 hours, which pleased me for my first race, but my legs were aching quite a lot.

I believe all the team finished, which was a good sign for our fitness, but I think that was when I got the bug, I wanted to run more races and improve my times. It was my ultimate goal to run a full marathon, and I wanted my first marathon to be London, which I was determined to do, but the selection process did not help. I kept being refused entry, but they then changed the rule, no doubt because there were many being refused entry, the new rule came into force. If anyone had been refused continually, they would gain entry on the fifth attempt, that was what happened to me, I was accepted in 1987, my fifth attempt. I remember the race quite well, it was very hard going, my legs started to hurt around 22 miles, but I finished in poor shape. It was fortunate that I had the next day off, I could not get out of bed, my legs had seized up, I knew the reason. I had not done enough work, I had not done enough mileage during training. At that moment I vowed to do the training for the race, I appreciated that without the training, it was going to be difficult to complete a marathon, I was not going to be caught out again. I continued to run half marathons, then someone suggested we run a half marathon from Amersham. I agreed to help with the organisation, along with several friends, we fixed a date, then we looked at what we needed. People needed to drink on the run, a colleague fixed up a bowser full of cold water, he also organised helpers from RAF Halton, they would hand out the water, along with wet sponges. The course itself was going to be a two-lap course, which means the water stations could be used twice. The biggest problem we had was for the course to be successful, we had to go up a steep hill, but this had to be done twice, I seemed to be in the habit of climbing steep hills. We had our committee, now we needed a famous person to start the race, that was when we were able to persuade Barbara Windsor, along with a local girl called Debbie Curtis. The money that we had hoped to make was to be donated to Amersham Town Football Club, they needed a new perimeter fence around the pitch. As far as I can remember we collected enough money for the job, there was quite a turnout for our first half marathon, we decided to make it an annual event, although the committee did not remain the same.

Myself and Alistair Shields preparing for the first Amersham Town Half Marathon, 1988.

It is now time to move onto my last police course, this was a continuation course at Ashford in Kent, it consisted of people from other forces, some of who I recognised from Eynesham Hall, the others I did not recognise.

The photograph shows our class, along with the sergeant instructor, it was an interesting course, the joy was there was no examination at the end. I am not sure how long we were there, it might have been a week, but I suspect it was a fortnight. It was another of those courses where you meet people for the first time, then you never see them again.

I now return back to my running, I tried for the London Marathon in 1989 and was accepted, then I realised the reason, because I had completed the race two years previously, I was expected to finish again. The London

Marathon wanted people to finish the race, hence my acceptance.

The photograph shows me completing the race in 4 hours and 2 minutes, but that was not my correct time, the start of the race has thousands of people crossing the start line, in this race, it took me 15 minutes to cross the start line, so my correct time was 3 hours and 47 minutes. I have marked me on the photograph just crossing the finishing line. I completed London again in 1991 and my final London Marathon was 1993. That final race was not by choice, I had problems with my right knee, it was strapped up doing that last marathon, I went in for an operation on my right knee a week later. I was hoping that I could run again after the operation, there were several marathons I was keen on competing in, one of those was Moscow, the other was the Great Wall of China. I do believe there was an Everest marathon, not so sure about that one. There were several other marathons I completed, I wanted to complete Berlin the year the wall came down, but I was unable to get in, I had to be satisfied running that one a year later. The thing I remember about that race, the majority of the race took place in what was East Berlin, that part of Berlin was very grey, there were no advertisements on the street, it was colourless apart from the grey. The streets were also littered with the Trebant car, which I believe had a plastic frame, it was the only car sold in East Berlin, people waited years to get one. I believe these cars were in great demand when the wall came down, but there was a problem with this car, if the owner was involved in an accident, the car folded up after a collision. I think there must have been a lot of careful drivers in East Berlin.

One of the best marathons to take part in was the Athens Marathon, which started at a famous place called Marathon, and finished in the original Olympic stadium in

Athens. The weather for the race was ideal, it drizzled throughout the race, keeping the runners cool. I enjoyed the race because the weather was favourable for running, but also for the historical value of the distance, and finishing in the original Olympic stadium, all these things added to the occasion.

Athens Marathon, 1988.
Outside the city of Athens.

Finishing in the original Olympic Stadium.

There was only one problem with the trip, it concerned taking a boat trip, the day before we were meant to fly home, this was something of a disaster. I went to a small island called Andros, it was a trip that took an hour, intending to return to the mainland a few hours later when I had seen the island. To my surprise, along with others who had made the trip, a storm erupted in great force, so much so that the boat was unable to sail back to the mainland. We were told we had to stay on the island overnight, which caused another problem, my flight was due to leave Athens airport the next morning. I telephoned the tour operator and explained the situation, they were very sympathetic, others on that flight had been stranded on different islands, so they made arrangements for me to stay in a hotel in Athens. I was then to take a flight back to the UK, but it was a case of waiting at the airport for a seat. We sailed back from Andros the following morning and went to the hotel in Athens, my back had already been taken there by the tour operators. Following a good nights sleep, I went to the airport, there were about a dozen people who had missed the flight, we waited for places on flights leaving for the UK, it depended on when you had arrived, there was a queue for seats. I was too far down the queue to get on the first few aircraft, so I waited with fellow passengers. Then we were told the next aircraft in was the last charter flight back to the UK, if we did not get a seat on that one, it meant paying for a seat with a normal airline, there was a lot of nervousness among the passengers. I believe there was only eight of us left to get on the flight, but I was the last arrival. The aircraft turned up and there was enough room for all of us, we boarded the aircraft and found it half empty, which meant we could stretch out, I enjoyed that flight back home.

Before I move onto other things to do with the police, there is one last marathon I need to mention. The trip was paid for by the MS unit in Aylesbury, it cost them £600, there was a proviso which I did not mind, I had to run for them, collect money for their cause, which I was glad to do. I in fact collected £1500, which I was pleased with. You are now wondering where the race was, it was in fact the New York Marathon.

I flew to New York a couple of days before the race, I stayed in Roosevelt Hotel on Madison Avenue, it was very close to Grand Central Station. Like all hotels in America, it was clean and I was well looked after. We had to go and register for the race, there we were given our number and a running vest.

On the day of the race we were transferred to Staten Island, that was to be the start of the race. I think that Staten Island can proudly say, on the day of the race, they had the longest urinal in the country, possibly the world. There were also places to buy food and drinks, we were there about an hour before the race started. The race itself was an experience, not only were the supporters very enthusiastic, but we passed through all the districts of New York, even those we would never have ventured into under normal circumstances. I do remember when we left Staten Island, we crossed the Verrazano Bridge to get us into New York, there were two separate roads on the bridge, one above the other. I went on the lower road, but quickly realised that those on the upper bridge were using it as a toilet, I decided to move away from the edge, everyone on the lower level made the same decision. As I said the event was well supported on the streets, leading to the finish in Central Park, it was a race I will never forget.

The next morning I went into a diner for breakfast, where I sat near two men who were talking about the race, but I think it is fair to say they never had the physique of runners, but they seemed to enjoy the race, I think many New Yorkers watched it on their televisions. I also ran in the Rotterdam and Venice marathons, but age and injury stopped me running anymore.

New York Marathon, 1989.
About to cross the finishing line.

I will now move onto the other great sporting event I attended, that being Royal Ascot. It was held in June and officers from Chesham were sent there, I was sent there with just over a year's service. I was sent there again a few years later. In the first year, I was on the gate of the unsaddling enclosure, all it meant was opening a large wire gate to let the first three horses in to be unsaddled, hence the name. When the horses were in there it was not unusual for the owners to come down and pat the horse, they also congratulated the jockey on a job well done. I thought very little of the job until Wednesday, I opened the gate, as usual, strolled the first three horses, I shut the gate. I looked over to where the horses were, there about 30 yards away was Her Majesty, her horse had been in the first three, I actually think it was the winner. She did not acknowledge my presence, not that I expected her to, but it would have been nice, that was going to be the closest I ever got to her, unless she intends to honour me with a knighthood. I never saw the Queen again in the unsaddling enclosure that week, perhaps it was her only winner. I enjoyed that week, along with seeing all the winning jockeys, many of whom I knew, mainly from watching television, not as you think from gambling. We were well looked after at Ascot, the food was good, I was looked after with drinks, non-alcoholic of course. I was offered the alcoholic type, unfortunately, I had to refuse, I had no idea if the Queen would turn up again, I wanted to be sober for that.

My second week at Royal Ascot, I believe it was two years later, we were in a place called the Silver Ring, it was very busy, and the crowd was very friendly. The popularity of the location was because we looked across the finishing line, it did not excite me too much, but the fans were cheering wildly as the race finished, I feel sure they did not all have the winner. It was there when a colleague spoke to a bookie on the track, he was willing to accept our bets, of course, he was, he was not bothered where his money came from. We did alright, I think we were up on the week. But the best day was to come, not because of the horse racing, Thursday was Ladies Day, and I am not talking about the hats. Some of the outfits were quite outrageous, but to a red-blooded male, they looked very good, particularly the ones in mini skirts. Once again we were fed well, we had our own building for our meals. I remember seeing a few well-known people there, Alan Ball and Mick Channon approached me, they had either lost their binoculars or had them stolen, we treated it as a theft. I also saw Robert Morley stagger from one of the bars, he appeared to be happy with his lot. I watched Ian Botham turn up, that was indeed a big man, both in height and a muscular width, he did not speak to me.

Another duty we had was the Reading Pop Festival, I got the impression it was a leftover from Greenham Common, the people were scruffy and unkempt, their tents were dirty and untidy, the only difference was that they were younger. Reading Pop Festival was a place for drugs, most used them, many of them sold drugs, arresting people for it was easy, they were open about it. The whole site smelt of cannabis, with good reason. We patrolled the site on foot, much to the disappointment of the drug users, there was a small hut to take those arrested, it was busy all the time. While on this patrol I looked across the river to the houses, I thought I saw two youngsters in the back garden, this was an ideal time to commit a burglary, most of the residents moved away during the festival. We called for the boat that was patrolling the river, it was called Sit Pax, it arrived quickly and we got on board, I directed the driver to the house. We got off and searched the garden and the perimeter of the house, we could not find our intruders, that was the most exciting part of the week.

The next important part of my career in the police was playing football, although it was a part-time involvement, usually on a Wednesday afternoon. These games were called Divisional Games, there were eight divisions, from a fixtures point of view it worked out quite well, as it did for cup games. Our division was not the top division, although we made it to two cup finals, winning one and losing the other, both were against Milton Keynes. There was another annual event, which unfortunately did not last very long. A colleague called Gerry Millett had passed away, he was a CID man at both Chesham and High Wycombe, so the fixture would be between those two teams of them, that was the original idea. I think we had played either two or three of these games, High Wycombe did not win any of these games, in fact, the last game they were beaten 7-0, as the picture shows. The man who organised the games was a High Wycombe CID officer, I know who he was but I will not mention him. He was not happy with these continual defeats, so he changed the format, only CID officers were allowed to play, I think High Wycombe won the next game, then the fixture was forgotten. Strange how people liked to get their own way, even if it meant changing the rules.

The Amersham team ready to play High Wycombe in the Gerry Millett Memorial Trophy,. We won the game 7-0.

We put a police team into the Wycombe Sunday league, and Chesham United allowed us to play our games at their ground, it was certainly better than other grounds we played at, but our existence in the league was short-lived. Because of the Miners Dispute, we were unable to fulfil our fixtures, we informed the league in the correct manner, but they would have none of it. We were not only thrown out of the league, but the league banned all the players Sine Die, which I believe means forever, there was a way back, but I cannot remember what it was. It is strange that a local Sunday League can exercise such power, they obviously thought it made them feel important. As a matter of interest, I am still banned by the Wycombe Sunday League, but it is fortunate that I am too old to play football anymore.

There is one further thing to mention, mainly because I have the relevant pictures. Like all policemen who have kept out of trouble for a period of 23 years, it was time to be presented with my long service medal, it was to be presented to me by the Chief Constable, at that time it was Sir Charles Pollard. The ceremony took place at Sulhamstead, all those eligible for the award turned up, it reminded me of something that was said in the first weeks of my service, it was the sergeant who was instructing us that said it. There were twenty of us that formed our course, then the sergeant made a statement, which I think surprised all of us, it was not what we wanted to hear. He told us that in the years to come most of us would leave, there would only be a quarter of us left to pick up the Long Service Medal. On that day at Sulhamstead there were only five of us left, exactly a quarter as predicted 23 years earlier. I received my medal, I was glad to have made it to the last five. After the presentation there were tea and cakes for all those present, which included our guests, it was a proud day, but I still thought of that prediction 23 years earlier.

2001. Chief Constable Sir Charles Pollard presenting me with my Long Servoce medal.

All those officers present received their Long Service medals. It was required to have completed 22 years of unblemished service.

Available worldwide from Amazon

---

www.mtp.agency

www.facebook.com/mtp.agency

@mtp_agency